Richelieu and Mazarin

IN THE SAME SERIES

General Editors: Eric J. Evans and P. D. King

LANCASTER PAMPHLETS

Richelieu and Mazarin

Geoffrey Treasure

London and New York

First published 1998
by Routledge
11 New Fetter Lane, London EC4P 4EE

Simultaneously published in the USA and Canada
by Routledge
29 West 35th Street, New York, NY 10001

Typeset in Bembo by
Ponting–Green Publishing Services, Chesham, Buckinghamshire
Printed and bound in Great Britain by
Clays Ltd, St Ives PLC

British Library Cataloguing in Publication Data
A catalogue record for this book is available from
the British Library

Library of Congress Cataloguing in Publication Data
Treasure, G. R. R. (Geoffrey Russell Richards)
Richelieu and Mazarin / Geoffrey Treasure.
p.   cm. – (Lancaster pamphlets)
Includes bibliographical references.
1. Richelieu, Armand Jean du Plessis, duc de, 1585–1642 –
Influence.   2. Mazarin, Jules, 1602–1661 – Influence.
3. Statesmen – France – Biography.   4. Cardinals –
France – Biography.   5. France – Politics and
government – 17th century.   6. Church and state –
France – History – 17th century.
I. Title   II. Series.
DC123.9.R5T73   1998
944'.032'0922–dc21
[B]   97–43863
CIP

ISBN 0–415–15354–9

Contents

Foreword

Lancaster Pamphlets offer concise and up-to-date accounts of major historical topics, primarily for the help of students preparing for Advanced Level examinations, though they should also be of value to those pursuing introductory courses in universities and other institutions of higher education. Without being all-embracing, their aims are to bring some of the central themes or problems confronting students and teachers into sharper focus than the textbook writer can hope to do; to provide the reader with some of the results of recent research which the textbook may not embody; and to stimulate thought about the whole interpretation of the topic under discussion.

Landmark dates

1619 First War between Marie de Médicis and Louis XIII
      (February–April)

1620 Second War between Marie and Louis; Peace of Angers
      (August); Mazarin in Spain (till 1622)

1621 Accession of Philip IV of Spain; Olivarez chief minister;
      end of Twelve Years Truce between Spain and United
      Provinces; death of Luynes in campaign against Hugue-
      nots (December)

1622 Richelieu becomes cardinal (September), and Provisor
      of the Sorbonne; Peace of Montpellier ends Huguenot
      war (October)

1624 Richelieu enters Council of State (April); La Vieuville
      dismissed, Richelieu becomes First Minister (August);
      Franco-Swiss army expels papal garrisons from Val
      Telline (November)

1625 Mazarin made captain in papal army

1626 Treaty of Monçon between France and Spain (March);
      execution of Chalais (August); Assembly of Notables;
      Richelieu's plan of reform (December)

1627 Siege of La Rochelle starts (September); death of duke
      of Mantua; Nevers claims succession

1628 Mazarin becomes secretary to papal nuncio, G.F.
      Saccheti; fall of La Rochelle (October)

1629 *Code Michau*; French invade Piedmont (March); Grace
      of Alais (June)

1630 Richelieu meets Mazarin at Lyons (January); Pinerolo
      captured by French (March); Richelieu's memorandum
      on Italian policy (April); Louis XIII ill (September);
      Treaty of Regensburg (October); Mazarin achieves truce
      of Casale (October); 'Day of Dupes' and fall of Marillac
      (November)

1631 Mazarin's first visit to Paris (January–February); Treaty
      of Bärwalde between France and Sweden (January);
      start of Renaudot's *Gazette*; Swedish victory at Breiten-
      feld (September); *Seigneurie* of Richelieu elevated to
      status of *duché-pairie*

1632 Treaty of Vic between France and Lorraine (January);
      Mazarin's second stay in Paris (April–July); Orléans-
      Montmorency revolt; execution of Montmorency (Octo-
      ber); death of Gustavus at Lützen (November)

widening breach over taxes and office-creation between crown and *Parlement*

1646   Crown imposes tariff on goods entering Paris (September)

1647   Treaty of Ulm between Bavaria and France (March); mutinies disrupt French campaigns

1648   Treaty of Münster between Spain and the United Provinces (January); *lit de justice* – Omer Talon's defiance (January); *Parlement's arrêt d'union* (May) followed by meeting of Chambre Saint Louis; Battle of Lens: Condé defeats the Spanish (August); arrest of Blancmesnil and Broussel (26 August) followed by Paris barricades; Treaties of Munster and Osnabrück comprise Peace of Westphalia (October); Declaration of Saint-Germain (October)

1649   Execution of Charles I (January); siege of Paris (January–April); Treaty of Rueil ends first *Fronde* (April); provincial conflicts continue: civil war in Guienne (starts in March) – Alais besieges Aix (July)

1650   Arrest of princes (January) – 'War of the Princesses' ensues; Gondi appeals for liberation of princes (December)

1651   Liberation of princes (January); Mazarin goes into exile (February); Condé breaks with Gondi and rebels (August); Louis XIV's Majority (September); Châteauneuf chief minister; Turenne returns to serve crown

1652   Mazarin returns (January); Châteauneuf dismissed, Gondi becomes cardinal (title, de Retz – February); Battle of Bléneau – Condé defeats royal army, enters Paris (April); Mazarin thanks Huguenots for loyalty (May); Battle of Faubourg St Antoine (July); *Ormeiste* coup in Bordeaux (9 July); French expelled from Catalonia; Mazarin's second exile (August); Louis XIV recovers Paris (October); arrest of Retz (December)

1653   Mazarin returns (February); Condé joins Spanish in Flanders; Bordeaux surrenders to crown (August); Fouquet appointed *surintendant*; Pope Innocent X declares Jansenist 'Five Propositions' heretical

1654   Louis XIV's coronation; Retz escapes from gaol (August); Turenne relieves Arras (August)

1655   Louis forbids *Parlement* to obstruct royal edicts;

Mazarin's commercial treaty with Cromwell, later (March 1657) enlarged into military alliance

1656   Spain makes alliance with exiled Charles II; first of Pascal's *Lettres provinciales; lit de justice* secures registration of Papal bull

1657   Ferdinand III dies, Leopold elected Emperor. Noble 'conspiracies of forest' (summer)

1658   Battle of Dunes (June) – Turenne, with English, defeats Spanish (and Condé); Portuguese defeat Spanish at Elvas; treaty between France and Brandenburg; League of the Rhine (August)

1659   Louis XIV renounces Marie Mancini; Peace of Pyrenees between France and Spain (November)

1660   Louis XIV marries Maria Teresa, Infanta of Spain (June)

1661   Mazarin dies (9 March)

Introduction

On 29 January, 1630, Cardinal Richelieu first met the young Italian diplomat, Guilio Mazarini, at Lyons. The latter's mission was to explain that his master, the Pope, wanted peace in North Italy. Richelieu's prime concerns were to secure his position at home and to take advantage of the Mantuan succession dispute by establishing French garrisons across the Alps. Thirteen years later the Italian took his seat at the table of the French royal council. Richelieu had not expressly declared, on his deathbed, that he wished Mazarin – as by now Frenchmen were calling him – to succeed him as *premier ministre*. He had however commended him to the king as the man most suited to carry his complex diplomacy through to a favourable conclusion. Richelieu could not have known that Mazarin would be in office, as he had been, for 18 years, nor that he would be successful, beyond all expectations, in establishing the primacy of France in Europe.

The regime of the Cardinals, 1624–61, had a profound effect on French government and society. In both foreign and domestic policies there was an essential continuity. The *Fronde* brought disruption, with temporary retreats and reversals; but its failure actually restored the trend towards absolutism and reinforced its principles. The relationship forged between the elder statesman and the young diplomat had been one of mutual respect. Yet it is the dissimilarities between the two men that are most

1

striking. If Richelieu's ascent to power was impressive, it could be explained at each stage in terms of family tradition and personal ability. Mazarin's, by contrast, seems to have something of the adventurer about it, with much of the fortuitous, and the man, at every stage, defying the odds. This study will be mainly concerned with the ways in which Richelieu and Mazarin understood their role, the ways they exercised power and the use they made of it. Understanding must start, however, with a study of the circumstances of their early years and their distinctive paths to power.

1
Two Paths to Power

Armand-Jean du Plessis de Richelieu was born in 1585. Two god-parents were marshals of France. His father François was Grand Provost at the court of Henry III from 1578 to Henry's death in 1589, with wide responsibilities for police and administration. More king's man than *dévôt* he then served Henry IV and fought strenuously at his side. His mother, Suzanne de la Porte, came from a prominent family of lawyers. One Richelieu great-uncle was a distinguished soldier, another, Antoine 'the monk', was notoriously dissolute and cruel. Nobility, service at court, soldiering, finance, office-holding and magistracy contributed to Richelieu's family tradition; the licensed violence of the years of civil war provided uncomfortable memories. François died in 1590, leaving his extensive affairs in confusion, a debt-burdened estate and a modest château at Richelieu where Armand-Jean spent his early years. After 1594 Poitou was for vacations, Paris for education. As the third brother he was expected to pursue a military career. After the Collège de Navarre, he therefore went to the fashionable academy of Antoine de Pluvinel to acquire the martial arts. But when the bishopric of Luçon fell vacant, and his brother Alphonse disqualified himself by becoming a Carthusian monk (1602), he agreed to forgo sword for mitre.

He had already shown his intellectual ability. Now he showed the focused ambition and self-discipline that would set him

3

apart. He returned to the Collège de Navarre and embarked on an intensive study of theology and philosophy. Since he was still under the canonical age he went to Rome for dispensation (1607) and impressed the authorities by his erudition and eloquence. Luçon had been in the gift of Richelieu's family since 1584 but he was the first bishop, since then, to reside. He spent only five years there (1608–13, with a few months in 1617) but he made an impact on the life of the diocese. He restored the near-ruined cathedral, visited his parishes, laid down strict rules for the conduct of clergy, introduced diocesan synods, founded a seminary, invited Capucin friars to found a hospice, struggled to improve relations with the Cathedral chapter and compiled a catechism which anticipated his more ambitious *Instruction du chrétien* (1618). A strenuous reformer in the spirit of the Council of Trent, it is likely that, at first, he envisaged promotion in the church rather than political office. It was the anarchic conditions that followed the assassination of Henry IV and which characterised the minority of Louis XIII under the regency of his mother Marie de Médicis that brought him directly into high politics.

There was a demand for a States-General. It met in 1614. Richelieu was chosen as a deputy for the First (ecclesiastical) Estate. Through the influence of Marie, and with the support of the scholar-diplomat Cardinal du Perron, he was chosen to speak on behalf of the church at its closing session. His message was pointed and timely: clergy should have a share in the government of the kingdom. The more *les grands* – notably Guise, inheritor of the tradition of the League, Rohan, the Huguenot leader, Vendôme, the king's half-brother and Condé, his cousin, the greatest and most demanding of them all – pressed their own claims, the more they advertised their unfitness for the highest office. Successive 'treaties' like that of Loudun in May 1616, exploited their power to bargain and impoverish the royal treasury. It was sound political instinct, therefore as well as an eye to the main chance that prompted Richelieu to risk cultivating Marie's energetic Florentine favourite, Concino Concini.

Richelieu was appointed almoner to Anne of Austria, Louis XIII's Spanish bride. Neither that strategic position nor his mother's favour endeared him to the adolescent king. In November 1616, he was appointed Secretary of State, with special

4

responsibility for foreign affairs and war. When, in the following April, a palace coup overthrew Concini, the young bishop lost office. In the face of the prejudice of the king and hostility of his minister-favourite, the duc de Luynes, he had to accept internal exile, withdrawing, first to Luçon, then to Avignon. It took patience and assiduous attention to Marie's interests to restore his political fortunes: all depended on the queen mother's position and the support she was able to rally among sympathetic nobles. Mediation between Marie and the royal government, leading in 1619 to the 'treaty' of Angoulême and the formal reconciliation of mother and son, provided him with the basis he needed.

Richelieu was acquiring a formidable reputation, *'tout puissant dans son esprit'* as one contemporary described him. Steadily he established contacts and built the *clientèle* without which he could not aspire to high office. Family and friends played their part. His sister Nicole was married to Urbain de Brézé, future governor of Anjou. The Bouthillier family and the Capucin friar Joseph du Tremblay served him with a devotion that suggests the power of his personality. He brought with him the idea of *fidelité* – familial, regional and feudal – which could bond men in loyal service beyond the basic motives of ambition and material reward: in that respect he was a good Poitevin. He was also driven by the fear of isolation. In 1618 his brother Henri's wife and only son died; in 1619 Henri was killed in a duel. If the family were to be 'considerable' (a recurring theme of his correspondence) it was all now up to him .

In these years he had to perform a delicate balancing act between the *dévôts*, like the Oratorian Bérulle, who looked to him to enhance the influence of the church, and the *politiques*, who were alarmed by the growing strength of the Habsburgs; so he was cautious in pronouncements about policy. He was aware, however, from the outset, of the importance of propaganda. The 'political nation' – those French men and women who were concerned about the affairs of church and state – were not numerous, but they created the climate of opinion in which a statesman had to operate. Outwardly he kept his distance from the *politiques*, but their leading publicist, François Fancan recruited fellow writers in Richelieu's interest, discussed affairs regularly with him, and wrote vigorous pamphlets, strongly anti-Spanish in tone. 'Listening a great deal', as he wrote in his

Testament, Richelieu was already amassing information, studying contemporary sermons and pamphlets, and courting public opinion. Perhaps it was this aspect, as much as his association with the queen mother, that Louis XIII sensed (without recognising its constructive side) when he said to Luynes: 'There goes the double-dealer'. Luynes was implacably opposed to him. It was therefore fortunate for Richelieu that the minister-favourite died, besieging Montauban, in December 1621.

When Richelieu became a cardinal (1622) it meant more than preferment within the church. He acquired a double status: principal representative of the interests of the church; principal too, in Rome's eyes, in the formulation of royal policies as they affected the church. It would give him precedence when he rejoined the royal council. Meanwhile he could afford to wait for ministers to fumble. No minister, since the fall of Sully (1611), had matched his grasp of affairs. Villeroi was more courtier than statesman, Sillery essentially a bureaucrat. Luynes' death left something like a vacuum in power. In January 1623 La Vieuville, competent in finance, and ambitious to move from the *surintendance* to overall control of policies, courted the queen mother. She had her own agenda. In April 1624, Richelieu entered the council. La Vieuville antagonised both Louis and Marie and floundered between policies, then in August, offered to resign. Louis had him arrested and asked Richelieu to act as *premier ministre*.

Throughout, it is Richelieu's single-mindedness in the search for influence and power that is most striking, along with the spirit of mastery to which he could now give full expression. Vieuville's fate provided an object lesson: he had assumed the role of chief minister but without the political arrangements needed to govern effectively. Richelieu's own varied experience had led him to accept what Bergin calls 'the political arithmetic of the age of Concini and Luynes', to realise that effective power must have, besides office and property, a defensible base, with large resources and potent allies: it was the spirit of the *place de sûrete*, the product, as for the Huguenots, of brutal civil wars. He had learned so much of the hazards and obstacles along the road to power that he would reserve for his writing the logic and clarity of thought that were so important to him as an intellectual. In the formulation of policy he would prove to be empirical; in its execution cautiously selective.

Guillo Mazarini was born in July 1602, the eldest son of Hortensia Bufalini: her family was noble, originally Umbrian. His father, Pietro, was Sicilian by birth but a Roman in career and concerns. He was major-domo to the eminent Colonna family. A Mazarini uncle was a renowned Jesuit and Guilio was educated at the Jesuit college in Rome where men noted his 'fine spirit, capacity and gracious manners.' He was marked out for preferment but sought it not as a Jesuit but in diplomacy. He moved confidently among the patrician families. He went to Spain, as tutor-companion to Giralamo Colonna. Even more important, as patrons, were the Barberini brothers, Francesco and Antonio, nephews and ministers to Matteo Barberini, who became Pope Urban VIII in 1623. Relations were sometimes strained, notably after 1631, as Francesco came to see Mazarini as the tool of France, but Mazarini's dedication to the interests of Cardinal Antonio, a lavish patron of the arts, would prove invaluable.

The advance of Catholicism in Germany could only be welcome to Rome. The Spanish grip on North Italy was another matter. The object of Papal diplomacy was to hold the balance between Bourbons and Habsburgs. In the 1620s that meant measures to counteract the dominance of the Habsburgs as they swept all before them in the first decade of what would be known as the 'Thirty Years War'. It was in that climate that Mazarini acquired his experience of the political world. Gian-Francesco Saccheti, Papal commissioner, secured him a commission in the regiment raised to guard the Val Telline pass. To the Saccheti family too he owed his steady rise, by way of special assignments, to the Papal legation that was to be crucial in his career. In 1629 he was given full powers to treat with the Spanish and French generals manoeuvring on behalf of their political masters, Olivarez and Richelieu. The theatrical coup by which, in October, 1630, he prevented imminent battle, brandishing before the opposed armies the text later formalised in the Treaty of Cherasco, brought Mazarini Euopean fame.

Though his career was now supported by a canonry, the kind of church endowment which Popes used to maintain favoured agents, Mazarini was still essentially the elegant cavalier. Good looks and courteous manners ingratiated him when his duties took him to the courts of France and Savoy. By 1634, when he made his first visit to Paris, as nuncio, he was seen by Spain as the accomplice of Richelieu. His papal brief was to prepare the ground for a general peace settlement. The victorious campaigns of Gustavus Adolphus, subsidised by Richelieu, had altered the balance of power. So his missions, on behalf of Richelieu, to resolve matters in the strategically sensitive duchies of Savoy and Lorraine, brought hostility in Madrid and the coolness at Rome which led, in 1636, to his temporary removal to the papal city of Avignon. It was an uncharacteristic time of despair for an ambitious, uncommonly resourceful man.

After the death, in December 1638, of Richelieu's confidant and agent, Father Joseph, the Cardinal needed a man on whom he could rely for diplomatic missions requiring subtlety and tact. Those qualities were required in the years before his final commitment to French service, when he was, in effect, serving two masters and a false move could have brought disgrace or eclipse. The Pope was affronted by Richelieu's alliance with Protestant powers and pressed by the Cardinal's *dévôt* critics to check Mazarini's ascent. But, as Habsburg armies faltered and the need for peace became more urgent, he realised that he could not afford to antagonise the French king. So, in January 1639, he acceded to Louis' request that Mazarini be made a Cardinal.

By December 1639, when he was able to respond to the formal invitation to come to France, Mazarin – as we should now call him – knew the diplomatic scene as well as any man. He had shown that he could hold his own with veteran generals, build relationships through good offices and timely gifts, serve patrons and win friends in the required manner. Soon he would have to contest control with men like Chavigny, Richelieu's *créature* and specialist in foreign affairs. Meanwhile he cultivated Chavigny's alliance. It was in these years too that he won the support of Louis XIII's Spanish wife, Anne of Austria whom, because of her sympathy for the *dévôts*, Richelieu had kept under close surveillance.

Increasingly frail, working relentlessly for the defeat of Spain, Richelieu might tease the suave Italian; but he became convinced of his worth and came to see him as indispensable. When, in Richelieu's last months, Mazarin showed the sympathetic concern that seemed, calculation aside, to come naturally to him, he cemented the all-important friendship. By the time he acted as a witness to Richelieu's will, he knew what huge wealth and influence could be got by one who could act in the sovereign's name. In the manoeuvres that followed Richelieu's death (December 1642) he showed that he was well versed in the mechanics of power. Richelieu has recommended that Mazarin be admitted to the council. It is likely that he envisaged him playing a leading role in peace talks; unlikely though that he saw him as *premier ministre*. As cardinal, like Richelieu before him, Mazarin could claim precedence in council. As an apparently disinterested adviser he could play on the king's suspicion of any minister who might look to dominate. So he secured the downfall of war minister Sublet de Noyers and the isolation of Chavigny, and was well placed, on the king's death (May 1643), with Anne's support, to assume the prime place.

2

Royal Servants

As *premier ministre*, Richelieu, like Mazarin after him, exercised power in the king's name. Sovereignty was royal, undivided, absolute. In his treatise *De la Souveraineté du Roy* (1612), Le Bret sets the king firmly on the plinth of Divine Right: holding his authority from God, without intermediary, he is accountable only to Him. No minister, no court, not even *Parlement*, could enjoy more than a delegated power. 'Sovereignty is no more divisible than a point in geometry'. Le Bret was a learned jurist: echoing Bodin, he anticipated Bossuet. He was also Richelieu's man, serving him on various missions and in special courts, such as that which condemned Louis de Marillac to death. It is therefore interesting that he was strongly against despotism: the king had to exercise power with moderation. Le Bret envisaged cooperation between crown, sovereign courts, and Estates, as their common interest required. If that represented his master's voice, so surely did his idea of *lèse-majesté*, covering three forms: slander against the king, attacks on his life and conspiracy against the state.

As Richelieu's ministry was threatened by plots and his propaganda challenged by hostile critics like Matthieu de Morgues, high claims were made for the Cardinal himself. Silhon's *Ministre d'État* (1631) used him to exemplify the virtues required of the ideal minister. Louis XIII was ordained by God to represent His power and bring harmony to the land.

His minister, by implication sharing in the Divine commission, supremely intelligent, virtuous and reasonable, could not be constrained by ordinary moral standards when defending the realm against its enemies, at home or abroad. The higher the end, the wider the licence – and no end could be higher than service to God's lieutenant on earth. Here, if needed, was the theoretical ground for special courts, arbitrary imprisonments, espionage, diplomatic pretences, all, on this reading of his rights and powers, left to the minister's personal judgement of what was required. In practice Richelieu took care to ensure that his major decisions were authorised by the king.

Even when his place was taken by the chancellor the king was always, in theory, presiding over the council. That was also the case in a minority, when the young king might be represented by a regent: in Louis XIV's case, by Anne of Austria. Royal decrees had the force of law: no authority, other than the king, could cancel them. The king had a wide range of appointments in his gift, governorships and military commands, for example. As the brief careers of both Concini and Luynes had shown, the favoured minister could expect to be given numerous offices, honours and commands to reward him for service and enable him to consolidate his position in the face of disappointed rivals or offended grandees. There was always the possibility of a ruler's change of heart. In this respect Mazarin's position was different from Richelieu's. Louis XIV came to the throne aged five and was a minor until 1651: royal authority was therefore harder to exercise. After the outbreak of the *Fronde*, in August 1648, Mazarin had to cope with great obstacles and perils, but he could rely on the royal authority, whether exerted by Anne, or by the young king: indeed it alone stood between him and downfall.

Richelieu had to deal with a moody, unpredictable monarch, jealous of his authority; of uncertain health, wayward in affections and sensitive to slights; devout, committed to the good of his dynasty, harsh towards opposition. He was aware, however, that his minister commanded respect at home and abroad, that he was exceptionally gifted, and that he worked tirelessly to promote the security of the realm. Richelieu knew Louis' foibles and kept himself informed, through his own *créatures*, of the king's moods and affections. He also respected Louis' dutiful nature, his piety and sense of divine mission. So he took pains to explain his policies. At certain critical junctures, under extreme pressure, afflicted perhaps by migraine, he could verge on hysteria, resort to the threat of resignation: then Louis could seem the stronger man. 1630 was a particularly anxious year: the minister's position and policies were alike in jeopardy, the king seriously ill. Not until November, and the 'Day of Dupes', so-called because Richelieu's opponents were misled into thinking that he would be dismissed, was his power confirmed. In 1636, when the fortress of Corbie had fallen and Habsburg armies threatened Paris, Richelieu urged evacuation; Louis, the warrior-king, rode out to join his army. During his last year, when Louis appeared to be infatuated with Cinq Mars to the point of losing all sense of proportion, Richelieu was sufficiently concerned about his relationship with the king to issue a memorandum laying down the rules for their working relationship. It amounted to an ultimatum. Yet we may still wonder if Louis would have wished then to alter a word of what he had written in 1626: 'My trust in you is complete, and . . . I have never found anyone whose service has pleased me so much'. Throughout there were times when, as at the siege of La Rochelle (1627–8), with both men in their military element, they worked well together. All in all theirs was a remarkable partnership, a kind of friendship, grounded in each man's respect for the other's sphere of action, character and ideals.

The key to Anne of Austria's relationship with Mazarin is to be found in her experience of married life. She was Spanish and her friends numbered those who, wishing for peace before anything, appeared to Richelieu therefore, to be favouring Spain. She was also neglected by her husband, to the point of humiliation. Living, under surveillance, on the margin of power, she found sympathy from the Papal legate and appreciated his suave manners – and his ability to speak her native Castilian. In 1643, relishing relative freedom and real power, but keenly aware of her responsibilities, Anne found in Mazarin, Louis' godfather, the ideal political partner. Was he more than that? Probably not. She was a Habsburg, proud, imperious in temper, rigorous in religious observance. Her prime concern was her son and his secure succession to power. Mazarin, much admired by women, had either been exceptionally discreet or celibate by preference. There is much of sentiment and more than conventional courtesy in his attentions to women, little apparently

12

of passion. Anne's letters to him in exile, with coded passages and symbols, express a longing for his company and counsel. Together, they were essentially partners in a great enterprise, with mutual respect and gratitude to bind them.

As a minister Mazarin was less concerned than Richelieu with principle, less indeed of an intellectual in his approach. It was not until he had endured the onslaught of the *Mazarinades* that he took steps, belatedly, to present his case through his own pamphleteers: a serious neglect of what Richelieu had established as a vital arm of government. He built, however, on what Richelieu had established as the pattern of work and responsibility. Inevitably, his role evolved in response to changing circumstances. Richelieu had secured discharge, in 1626, from the duty of hearing private grievances in order that he could concentrate on matters of state. That had meant that he could choose his ground, decide whom to consult. It was a sign of growing authority that after 1630 he began to delegate, even in areas of policy which concerned him most: foreign affairs and war. With the mobilisation of resources for war had come the development of specialist departments, with trusted men, *créatures* like war minister Sublet de Noyers, taking independent decisions and creating their own *clientèles*. He was content to let his *surintendant* control all but the strategic aspects of financial policy. In all this Mazarin followed. As with Richelieu, diplomacy was an overriding concern. Much of his time was spent in reading and composing dispatches. Indeed, Mazarin's approach to domestic affairs was essentially that of a diplomat. At first, unpractised in its routines, he was hesitant in council. Aware that he was suspect as an Italian, still an outsider, his overriding concern was to avoid making unnecessary enemies. Yet magnates who looked forward, like La Rochefoucauld, to 'a slack regency' were disappointed; some, as in Richelieu's time, resorted to intrigue. For Mazarin was the prime mover of policy. It was he who issued instructions to governors, generals and ambassadors. As he grew wealthier he could extend his patronage. Michel Le Tellier, war minister after 1643, Nicolas Fouquet, *surintendant* from 1653, Jean-Baptiste Colbert, the faithful commissary, were loyal as well as able: to serve Mazarin was to ensure their future; meanwhile they in turn built their *clientèles*.

3

The Huguenot Question

To identify the obstacles to the effective wielding of royal
authority, Richelieu needed to look no further than his family
history and his own experience: the feud with a neighbouring
family that led to killings and his father's temporary disgrace;
his father's subsequent role at court, witness to degradation in
morals and politics, then serving under Henry IV in the last
stages of a civil war which saw the Spanish armies fighting in
northern France; his eldest brother killed in a duel; his own
dealings with the Huguenots in his diocese of Luçon, close to
La Rochelle; his participation in a States-General which had
exposed the conflicting interests of nobility and Third Estate; his
negotiations on behalf of Marie de Médicis when she was at
odds with her son. There were special circumstances. The last
Valois kings ruled feebly. Royal minorities tempted over-mighty
subjects to hold the crown to ransom. The fundamental causes
lay, however, in the structure of the realm in this period of
transition between Renaissance kingship, still largely a matter
of personal royal rights and influence, and the developed state
of Louis XIV's reign, when his law reached, through his *intendants*, to most corners of the land, and French armies were
effectively under his control. Within the sixteenth-century
patchwork of provinces, estates and cities, so diverse in laws,
customs, even language, the growth and consolidation of the
Huguenot party had revealed the crucial weakness of the state.

Because of the way in which the cause had been taken up by nobles, and the concessions which the crown had been forced to make in the Edict of Nantes (1598), it was clear that the question of authority was also a Huguenot question. When Richelieu was forced to withdraw French troops from the Val Telline in 1625 because of a Huguenot rising, he decided that he must strike: a decisive victory over the Huguenots would also send a message to others who defied the king.

By the terms of the Edict of Nantes, beside freedom to worship in specified places, to attend any schools and universities and to meet, for religious purposes, in assemblies – rights which exceeded those, for example, of Catholics in England – the Huguenots had won several of the rights that might be expected to belong exclusively to the crown. Special tribunals were established for trying lawsuits dealing with Huguenots. Most significantly, Huguenots were allowed to garrison, at the expense of the crown, certain towns, *places de sûreté*. The Edict represented compromises after a military stalemate. It did not mean that there was a state within a state; it implied only a conditional tolerance on the part of the state. After the Edict there had ensued a kind of cold war, punctuated by riots and risings, as each party sought to exploit its terms.

Huguenot risings have to be put in the context of the German war: in the 1620s Protestants everywhere were concerned about the fate of their German brethren after successive defeats, culminating in the battle of Lütter and defeat of the Danes (1626). Like their fellow Calvinists in Holland and Germany, Huguenots saw their own struggle for rights in the light of their theology: it was necessary to resist the unjust ruler. Such Louis XIII seemed to them when he launched his campaign of 1621, in crusading spirit, to crush the Huguenots of the south-west. Their leaders, La Force, Trémoille and Soubise, had provoked this action however by deciding, at an illegal assembly at La Rochelle, to defy the government. After initial successes, Louis' campaign was checked at Montauban. The siege of the town lasted from August to December while the royal army wasted away through sickness and desertion: a prominent death was that of Luynes. In October 1622, after further operations, both sides were relieved to sign the Peace of Montpellier. The Huguenots had been weakened. They had lost control of Lower Languedoc. La Rochelle was nearly isolated. A base for future royal action was established at Fort-Louis, commanding the landward approach to La Rochelle. When in May 1625, the town responded to Soubise's call to rebellion, it may have looked a favourable moment, since royal troops were embroiled in the Val Telline. On wider considerations it was ill-judged: the Protestant cause was jeopardised when Richelieu decided to withdraw his troops from the Val Telline. The treaty of Monzon (March, 1626) led to a temporary improvement in relations both with Spain and the Papacy, and therefore in Richelieu's standing at home: with *dévôts* in fervent support, he could turn to the constructive proposals of reform presented to the Assembly of Notables of 1626, and concentrate his military effort on the Huguenots of La Rochelle. After the defeat of Soubise at sea by Montmorency, intervention by English envoys and the patching up of a peace treaty in February 1626, the Rochelais became convinced that Richelieu was bent on destroying them and turned to the English for protection. An expedition under Buckingham besieged the fortress of St Martin on the Isle of Rhé. After its failure and his return to England, Louis and Richelieu proceeded with their blockade of the town.

A semi-circular line of fortification was constructed, linking each point of the bay of La Rochelle. A great mole was built across the entrance to the harbour. The effort was prodigious; the stakes could not have been higher. The example of Wallenstein before Stralsund had shown how difficult it was to besiege a seaport. The siege lasted a year. In October 1628 La Rochelle capitulated and a few thousand citizens awaited their fate. Mayor Guiton's courage earned respect, but the king, and some councillors, wanted stern measures: the siege had been expensive. Military convention was against Richelieu but he stood out for clemency. It is one of those episodes which set him apart from his colleagues and his age: a measure of greatness. The Rochelais were allowed to live, to keep their property and – despite the urging of the *dévôts* – their freedom of worship. Richelieu had secured the real advantages he had fought for: the town lost its fiscal privileges; it had to accept a growing Catholic presence. It was a signal victory, a demonstration of the will and strength of the crown, a lesson to would-be rebels. It fitted Richelieu's plans to develop a royal navy. The subsequent Edict of Alés (June, 1629), following the subjugation of the other Huguenot towns in the Midi, was not a treaty but a 'grace' or pardon. It stripped the Edict of Nantes, confirmed in most other respects, of those clauses which secured the Huguenots' political and military rights. The walls of 20 towns were destroyed. Watching the removal of the first stones from the walls of Montauban, Richelieu could reflect on a personal triumph. Historians have since stressed that it was a landmark in the messy, piecemeal process that was the evolution of the 'absolute' state.

The wisdom of Richelieu's policy was shown during and after the *Fronde*, when the Huguenots were given opportunities to rebel and extort concessions from a hard-pressed administration – but did not take them. Old fires still smouldered. In May 1643, a rumour that a mob was on its way to the chapel of Charenton was enough to cause the congregation to panic, while nobles stood by with drawn swords. In 1653 a quarrel over the building of a temple in the Rhône valley led to the setting up of an armed camp of some 6,000 men. A Huguenot was a ring-leader in the assemblies of noblemen that troubled Mazarin in the post-*Fronde* years. Violence always threatened. In the first years of the minority, Balthasar, *intendant* in Languedoc, proposing that Huguenots be excluded from office, might well have triggered the rising he feared. If any incident in the *Fronde* had roused Huguenots in the south-west, where the provincial *Fronde* was most active, the course and outcome of the *Fronde* would have been different. The head of the Rohan family had been treated with politic generosity by Richelieu; yet he joined the rebel Condé. The provinces where the Huguenots were most numerous, like Poitou and Saintonge, were those where Condé found most recruits; many of them were noble. Speakers in the Church Assembly repeatedly called for action against heresy. Mazarin was often condemned for cynical laxity. He had to steer a cautious path between political opportunism, which dictated caution, and responding to Catholic fervour. He was assisted by the trend within Huguenotism towards moderation, as figures prominent in the financial administration, like Hervart, appointed *contröleur-général* in 1657, or in artistic spheres, pursued successful careers. But the crucial fact that there was no general rising during the *Fronde*, so that the crown could officially thank the Huguenots for their loyalty, is witness to the good sense of Mazarin in sticking to Richelieu's moderate policy.

4

Noble Attitudes and Politics

A nobleman himself, Richelieu was sympathetic to the noble order, respectful of its values, and, within limits, of its privileges. Those limits were defined by his idea of the state. The nobility were 'the nerve of the state', the heart of the army, the embodiment of the principles of honour and loyalty: all these – but what kind of state? Whose army? What kind of loyalty? For Richelieu – and the idea came to permeate the royal administration – the state was embodied in the person of the king, to whom all were subject. The duty of the subject, noble or commoner, was to obey, unconditionally. The sovereign too had commitments. Absolute in theory, in practice he was constrained by the fundamental laws (concerning succession, for example), whose guardian was *Parlement*; also by the rights of bodies ranging from the church, Estates and *Parlements*, to provinces, towns and the legion of office-holders. Privilege, not in the modern, vaguely pejorative sense, but in that of acknowledged private law, was all-pervading. Most jealously guarded were the privileges of nobility: to have a coat of arms, to wear a sword and, in most cases, to be exempt from the *taille*. Many nobles were poor; always a few were losing noble status; among the richest some were of the *robe*, some of recent creation; at the summit were a handful of great families, *les grands*, mostly *ducs et pairs*; some had royal blood. Montmorency represented the summit of feudal hierarchy and service; Condé was a cousin

18

of the king, Vendôme an illegitimate son of Henry IV.

It was at that level, where a nobleman might regard himself as a prince, perhaps, like Bouillon, having lands outside the realm, family connections with the house of Orange and an independent *vicomté* in the south of France or, like Condé in the Clermontais, having the right to collect taxes, that noble power represented a threat to the state. That is where Richelieu can be seen – and so he claimed to have promised Louis XIII – as resolved 'to abase the pride of the nobles'. It did not inhibit him from building his personal empire so as to be the greatest among them, acquiring estates, honours and palaces and arranging strategic marriages, culminating in that of his niece, Claire-Clemence Brézé, to the duc d'Enghien, the 'great Condé' as he was to be.

Deeply ingrained in the aristocratic mentality was the idea of service to the king, the feudal superior; voluntary, personal, therefore conditional. There was the right, assumed by some families to be hereditary, to be governors of provinces. This entailed command of troops, extensive patronage, a local eminence even more dangerous when it went with large estates in the province. Such an accretion of political and economic power meant that the highest nobles had extensive *clientèles*, among officials as well as fellow nobles: men whose direct loyalty was to the great man, even if it came to armed rebellion. With the general assumption that the crown had a special obligation to protect the interests of the noble order, when a determination among the greatest to share in counsel, to have a visible stake in the affairs of the realm. With the Condés, for example, it weighed much, providing a clue to the great general's apparently self-absorbed course, first as servant, then opponent of the crown.

Such attitudes found expression in the persisting custom of duelling. It set the nobles apart, as being exclusively their practice. It cost many lives. The crown had made ineffectual efforts to stop the practice. Effective prohibition would make a significant statement about the crown's absolute power. When, in 1627, the comte de Bouteville, a member of the Montmorency family, openly defied a royal edict by staging a triple duel in the Place Royale, he was executed. Duelling was not stamped out but an important precedent had been set.

Richelieu's elevation and his resolute use of royal power,

ensured that there would be opposition and intrigue. Assassin-ation was always on someone's agenda. Each episode had its particular causes and concerns. To each a name is customarily given – that of a principal victim: Chalais in 1626; Marillac in 1630; Montmorency in 1632; Cinq Mars in 1642. A common factor was Gaston of Orléans, Louis XIII's brother, heir-presumptive until 1638. Chronically indecisive, he was prob-ably more dangerous to conspirators than to Richelieu. Chalais went from a short trial by a picked court to execution because he was drawn into a plot on Gaston's behalf. Gaston himself could not be touched, nor could the Vendômes, Louis' two half-brothers. Gaston could also be relied on to inform against those who supported him – or used his name for their ends. Louis de Marillac, a general serving in Italy, paid the penalty for assumed complicity in the abortive coup of November 1630 to replace Richelieu by his brother, Michel de Marillac. The latter died in prison. Louis was beheaded, in the place de Grève, in May 1632. Where evidence was lacking, *raison d'état* could be invoked: an unsound general, with an army, was potentially dangerous.

Marillac was not of the highest family; the duc de Mont-morency was. His family had given the crown five constables, seven marshals, five admirals. The name evoked images of gallantry, honour, and service in high feudal mode. He had been offended when Richelieu had deprived him of the Admiralty of France. His province bordered on Spain. His instinct was that of a loyal soldier. When Richelieu sought to impose *élections* on the province, Montmorency negotiated. He was, however, per-suaded to make common cause with Gaston, in self-imposed exile. An Orléanist pamphlet called Richelieu 'disturber of the public peace, enemy of the king and the royal family, destroyer of the state, usurper of all the best offices of the state. . .'. Did Gaston believe that such faults justified so dangerous a course? In September 1632 the combined army of Gaston and Mont-morency was defeated at Castelnaudary. Montmorency was wounded. For Richelieu the choice was hard. Anything short of execution would be seen as weakness, for Montmorency had committed high treason. Legally the duke could insist on trial by peers in the *Parlement* of Paris. The support of the king was vital here. He was resolute: 'he must die'. Against a storm of protest Montmorency was tried in the *Parlement* of Toulouse and executed. It was a decisive moment. Mazarin's approach would be more conciliatory. But it would assist him that the relation of subject to prince had been so clearly defined, through the fate of the greatest of subjects. 'All persons', wrote Le Bret, 'being equally subjects of the same king, are equally subject to the same law'. In his *Testament Politique* Richelieu himself contrasted the good a prince could do, if the public good were his sole end, with 'the evil that a state suffers when they prefer the interests of individuals to those of the public'.

Cinq Mars was the king's indulged favourite, promoted and endowed beyond his deserts: a reckless, insolent foe to the cardinal. By 1641 'Monsieur le Grand', as he was called, threatened Richelieu's position because he could manipulate the king: he exploited concerns about the cost of war; he could count, at the outset, on Gaston and Bouillon. Richelieu learned through spies that they were making a deal with Spain: a Spanish army was to invade; then peace would be made, with restitution of conquests. The principals came to heel when Richelieu offered them pardon – Bouillon in return for placing Sedan under French protection, Gaston for revealing all he knew. In September 1642 Cinq Mars was executed. Richelieu pressed the king further. He would resign if Louis did not promise never to take another favourite from outside the council. Louis complied.

Such episodes reveal more than particular grievances and ambitions. An issue throughout was Richelieu's foreign policy. Subsidies to Protestant powers, and then, after 1635, open war against Spain, were seen by many, not only the most zealous *dévôts*, to be a gross abuse of royal authority, wrong in Catholic principle and disastrous in social effects – through oppressive taxation leading to disturbances and revolts, and the enrichment of the few at the expense of the many. Richelieu's wealth and power earned respect and execration in equal measure. Foremost among his critics was Marillac, Keeper of the Seals until 1630, and prime author of the *Code Michau* (1629). He was no less absolutist, indeed he was more dogmatic, when it came, for example, to limiting the rights of *parlements* in relation to the crown. He was less committed to the expansion of the realm, more to the well-being of the people and to the *dévôt* programme for the conversion of Huguenots. The argument did not die with his death. It was only intensified when Mazarin succeeded Richelieu and continuity seemed to be the order of the day: an unpopular war, unprecedented levels of taxation, increasingly arbitrary measures and a sense, not confined to a few nobles or *parlementaires*, that society was out of joint – and he an alien, without a significant *clientèle*. All these factors point to the enormity of the challenge and add to the significance of Mazarin's achievement.

The derisively named plot, *Cabale des Importants* (1643), was tracked by spies and was abortive. In its mixture of grievance, ambition and principle it links the opposition to Richelieu to the general disorder of the *Fronde*. At its heart was the faction of Vendôme. The duc de Mercoeur represented the interest of his father who had been deprived by Richelieu of the governorship of Brittany. His younger brother, Beaufort, thinking himself 'to be Mars and Adonis' (Mazarin) represented mainly himself, archetype of the reckless gallant who stood to gain by disorder. Five years in the Bastille was his punishment. Under Richelieu it would probably have been death. Mazarin enjoyed – and needed – good luck. He escaped the assassination that Beaufort planned. His ministry began with news of Condé's great victory over the Spanish at Rocroi (19 May, 1643). There was glory indeed – but the greater frustration when it was not followed by peace.

5

War: A State of Emergency

The revolts and plots of noble factions are only the most prominent aspect of opposition to the cardinals. In the case of Montmorency the wrecking tendency was enhanced by provincial antipathy towards Paris and support among local officials. Richelieu's executions and purges, his steady policy of securing control in the provinces by putting new, presumed loyal men into governorships, exhibited his power in the most visible way. It was only one aspect of a trend in government which threatened a permanent change in the balance between crown and subjects. The growth in the use of *intendants* was to be the prime grievance of the *frondeurs*, linking for a time the interests of nobles with those of officers of law and finance.

In origin *intendants* were royal agents on special mission. Under Henry III and Henry IV, *maîtres des requêtes* were dispatched to provinces on tours of inspection to examine this, regulate that, according to need. Between 1560 and 1620 about 120 were appointed. More intensive use came in the 1630s with the fiscal demands of war: it was 'the decisive factor in the establishment of the *intendants*', according to Bonney. By 1642 they were to be found in all the *pays d'élections*. They were, typically, young Parisians, *Maitres des Requêtes*, sufficiently ambitious to risk health and reputation in arduous work: they would have bought their judicial office, but they could not buy this crown appointment: they usually served three years before transfer; they served the king, in practice his *premier ministre* or chancellor, not the community to which they were sent. If they did well they could look forward to promotion, even a ministerial career. Particelli d'Hémery and Michel le Tellier were two whose careers took off in this way. *Intendants* were expected to work with the governor, but to keep an eye open for subversive activity. In frontier provinces they were to work alongside the general, with responsibility for supplies, pay and billetting. They were often resented, particularly when they began to take over the raising of taxes.

At times *intendants* found themselves threatened by local risings. In one form or another, *taille, aides, gabelle*, the crown's levies, always short of what war demanded, always rising inexorably to the limits which communities could stand, were the prime cause of urban disturbance, like those of 1630 in Dijon and Aix, and the more serious peasant risings. They were not a new phenomenon. There had been eruptions in the sixteenth century, some, latterly, the consequence as much of the collapse of civil order as of oppressive rule. But the *Croquant* risings of 1636, spreading from the Angoumois to Périgord, were more extensive and serious than any preceding outbreaks. They exposed the brutal dilemma of a war government trapped within a chronic state of emergency. The crown could not raise more taxes without provoking revolts which would involve both costs and loss of revenues: hence more direct intervention in the fiscal process and thereby further incitement to resist or rebel.

The *Croquants* did not express any deep antagonism towards their *seigneurs*; on the contrary the peasants seem to have looked to them for leadership, and sometimes to have found it. Surviving manifestos express the peasants' loyalty to the king, inevitably, therefore, hostility to the evil deceptions of his ministers. The immediate target was the tax system and its agents. In the Saintonge the peasants identified the double process as they linked extortion and rule from the centre: '*Parisiens et traitants*' were responsible for their ruin. The king, they imagined, was unaware of their plight. '*Vive le roi sans la gabelle!*'. '*Mort aux maltôtiers* [or *gabeleurs*]'. The words might vary with circumstances. Unmistakeable everywhere are the desperation, outrage, even sense of betrayal. Sometimes tax officials were murdered and mutilated. In the last resort the peasants gathered in large armed bands to fight for their cause.

Some, old soldiers or deserters, had military experience. At a crucial phase of the Spanish war, regular soldiers had to be sent in. That in itself was usually sufficient. There was only one general engagement of any importance when, at La Sauvetat, in 1637, La Valette defeated a larger peasant force and inflicted a thousand casualties.

The *Croquant* risings made the collection of taxes virtually impossible. When it was resumed it was usually under the guard of fusiliers. In diversion of troops and lost revenues the risings had a serious impact. They did not, in themselves, threaten to overturn the government. As in the *Fronde*, the particularism of the country which made it so hard to govern served also to preserve government from the ultimate threat: a general and concerted rising. Each province had its own character and concerns. The revolt of the *Nu-pieds* of Lower Normandy in 1639 did not even win the support of the rest of the province. Fear and antipathy governed the response of towns to peasants. A few nobles, some priests, gave a lead; most stood back. As for the greatest in the land, whatever their own grievances, peasant risings served to recall them to a sense of responsibility for good order.

The government's reprisals after the suppression of the *Nu-pieds* were directed by the Chancellor, Pierre Séguier in person. His unprecedented severity shows what had most alarmed ministers about a revolt which was prompted by rumours concerning the extension of the *gabelle*: the complicity of local officials. Such men had already seen their offices devalued by the additional creations which were now a mainstay of royal finance. The sale of office raised an average of 20 million *livres* a year during Richelieu's ministry. The treatment of Normandy may reveal a measure of desperation in ministers. It also shows the sternest face of absolutism. Richelieu was determined to teach the province a lesson which would be heeded by the rest of France, especially by its most influential townspeople. Officials were dismissed, the *Parlement* of Rouen was suspended for three years, fines amounting to more than a million *livres* were exacted from the towns.

The emergencies of war had created a 'fiscal terrorism' (Bercé). They also brought an unprecedented intrusion on the rights of local officials. In 1637, *surintendant* Bullion, under pressure from Richelieu, ordered *intendants* to see that towns paid the forced loan that was the government's latest response to the shortfall in receipts of the *taille*. The next step was to farm the receipts from the taille. In August 1642 the government adopted the most extreme and radical course. The assessment of the *taille* was transferred to the *intendants*, with overriding authority over *élus* and *trésoriers*. Soon *receveurs* were being replaced by the agents of the tax farmers. Everywhere officials of the traditional administration were being shoved to the margin, losers both in prestige and purse. The object was plain: to make the levy fairer and to secure more of it. It was not to lighten the overall burden. It all amounted to a momentous advance of government, but one which would not go unchallenged.

The *Fronde* would begin with the resistance of *Parlement* and the other sovereign courts to the financial demands and arbitrary measures of the crown. It may seem that Richelieu managed *Parlement*, and the provincial *parlements* more skilfully than his successor.

Since Richelieu had grown up within the system it was to be expected that he would have an instinctive sense of rights and limits. Advancing and retreating, turning political reverses to financial advantage, capable of longer views and plans, but driven necessarily to settle for immediate gains, he held sternly to his main course. Since he bequeathed a situation close to bankruptcy, it can be said that troubles were not resolved, but deferred. There was impressive firmness, with a touch of bullying; there were also more compromises than might at first appear. In his writings Richelieu liked to appear the omniscient physician of the state: the maladies clearly diagnosed, the remedies administered without flinching. The further one goes from the author to the statesman the more one becomes aware of a paramount fact: he was a great survivor.

6

A Limited Absolutism

Parlements, like the other sovereign courts, claimed to be 'sovereign' because they were derived from the mediaeval Curia Regis and partook of royal authority. With jurisdiction stretching over a third of the country, the *Parlement* of Paris was the most important, enjoying the right to register edicts, to examine and therefore to remonstrate. To point out faults in a law, something which clashed with precedent or was harmful to the state, gave scope for opposition – but not the right to reject. If the king wished an edict to become law, *Parlement* could do little to delay its registration. The social dimension was also important. The judges of *Parlement* were at the summit of the *noblesse de robe*, a legal aristocracy. They were rich, and usually had estates round the capital. In their courts on the Île de la Cité they had the sense of being at the heart of affairs, as they were of the city, and of belonging to a privileged and exclusive club, entrusted with the care of the traditional rights and usages of the realm. Offices had become hereditable property, secured by purchase in a way now regularised by the *paulette*. Possessing this considerable investment in a limited market, *parlementaires* saw to it that their own rights were secure.

A conservative oligarchy, with a radical fringe among its younger members, *Parlement* was likely to be in sympathy with the crown in its primary function of maintaining the order and security of the realm, but tenacious of its privileges. It tended to be cooperative if monarchy were strong and its demands did not infringe on *Parlement*'s undoubted rights and perceived responsibilities. One reason why *Parlement* was reluctant to register the *Code Michaud* was that it saw in Richelieu's proposal to let the lesser nobility into certain administrative positions, in colonial affairs for example, an attack on its privileged position. It had already tried to block Richelieu's appointment to be *Grand Maître et Surintendant de Commerce*. If monarchy were weakened, as during a regency, or in civil war, then it would be more assertive and adopt a political stance. The right of registration then became a weapon, a chance to attack royal policy or appointments. For Richelieu, relations with *Parlement* were soured by the crown's hunger for revenue, but he could rely on a sovereign who would brook no questioning of his authority. Mazarin, under the same financial pressures, in a minority, then a civil war, had to rely more on tactical manoeuvres and the personal dealings in which he excelled, but which tended to arouse mistrust.

The king could fall back on the *lit de justice*, a special session at which he would be present to enforce registration. Its occasional use only increased *Parlement*'s determination to defend its privileges. To use it, as Louis did in 1629, simply when he became impatient, was to exacerbate feeling in a situation always, potentially, one of conflict. For a century the crown had sought to guard a political exclusion zone, to preserve in matters of state policy, its freedom to decide. When Michel de Marillac informed magistrates that their role was to dispense justice, not to deal with matters of state, or Louis XIII informed a *parlementaire* deputation that they were there 'only to judge master Peter and master John' (January, 1632), they were following the example of Francis I, who had forbidden *Parlement* to interfere in state matters (1527). 'If you continue your machinations, I will cut your nails to the quick': Louis XIII's brusque words might have hurt less if magistrates had not felt that they were under attack within their own sphere of law.

A distinctive feature of Richelieu's government was his use of special courts and commissions. The trial of Michel de Marillac, Montmorency and Cinq Mars were essentially political trials: the verdict was predetermined by the minister's selection of judges. He went further, with the creation of the notorious chambre de l'Arsenal for the trial of political offenders: he used it in conjunction with special agents for surveillance and swift action. Richelieu would justify it in terms of *raison d'état*, as when, in the aftermath of the *Nu-pieds* rising, men were executed without trial, or as in the imprisonment of Saint-Cyran. In the Chancellor, Pierre Séguier, *dévôt*, absolutist in temperament and training, Richelieu had the ideal aide. When the issue of arbitrary imprisonment was raised during the *Fronde*, his words might have been written by Richelieu: 'When persons can disturb the tranquillity of the state through cabals . . . though their cases cannot be proved, formalities are useless'. He was always ready to sanction the diversion of cases from *Parlement* to the royal council and lend the authority of his office to political justice. *Raison d'état* represented the critical difference between the traditions represented by *Parlement* and the new royalist thinking and ministerial style. Its premise was that the king, divinely ordained, was endowed with unique qualities and rights. In matters of justice he decided according to royal rules distinct from those of any subject. To borrow Charles I's memorable scaffold phrase – 'subject and sovereign were clean different'.

'More affairs are decided by commissions than by ordinary judges.' There were principles at stake. But this *parlementaire*'s view reflects material interests: a loss of fees as well as of prestige. Moreover the value of offices was affected by the crown's regular creations of new offices. The motive in 1635, after the start of the war against Spain, was simply financial. Louis held a *lit de justice* in December to register edicts creating new offices. Members of the *Enquêtes* sought a plenary session: leaders were arrested and banished; their colleagues declared a strike; the king agreed to reinstate the banished members and to reduce the number of new offices from 24 to 17. In 1638 the same sequence of events followed the government's failure to honour *rentes*. The crown won without ceding anything. But the *rentes* issue broadened the scope for conflict for many *parlementaires* were also *rentiers*.

Richelieu's policies were driven by the unprecedented financial demands of war. By 1642 he was reduced to by-passing the established financial regime. In the same spirit he assaulted the rights of those provinces, *Pays d'États*, where the *taille* was raised on the basis of property and the Estates were responsible for its amount, allocation and collection. Inevitably they paid less. Much, arguably, was to be gained by introducing *élections*: a higher tax yield, money from new offices and a more direct political control. In 1628 a royal edict created ten *élections* in Dauphiné, with 270 officials: resistance overruled, their Estates died. Burgundy too lost its privileges (1630), but only after resistance and rioting in Dijon. In Provence too there was violence. The tone of local feeling can be gauged by the Estates' protest: the setting up of *élections* was 'the most prejudicial thing, not only in regard to the goods,but also to the liberties, even the very lives of the inhabitants of this *pays*'. A similar assault on the rights of Languedoc contributed to local support for Montmorency's rising. Brittany was left alone, probably because Richelieu knew its spirit and wanted nothing to upset his strategic concerns in the province.

It is arguable that it was Marillac, rather than Richelieu, who was most concerned about establishing fiscal uniformity. Certainly, after his downfall, compromise was the order of the day. Was it less a matter of ministerial priorities than of fast-changing circumstances? Richelieu was never a man to ignore realities. Much of remoter France was seething with discontent; meanwhile the costs of war mounted alarmingly. To alienate local officials was to add to the dangers of popular risings: the ministerial nightmare was of such a rising provoked and led by local officials. A safer policy was to wield a big stick, then accept money in return for concessions. In Burgundy, Provence and Languedoc the new *élections* were therefore abolished. 'Compensation', in the case of Languedoc was nearly four million *livres*. The immediate fiscal advantage of the *élections* had been less certain. *Élus* were notoriously corrupt. Soon government would be turning to a different method, that of sending out its *intendants* to control the process.

Richelieu's strategic vision was grand and his commitment to the defeat of Spain unwavering. To this end royal authority had to be sustained. He saw tax-raising simply as a means to that end; the forms of institutions, and the rights of their members, as secondary to the need for cash in hand. It is important, again, to distinguish between Richelieu the political philosopher and literary artist, and Richelieu the embattled statesman, empirical and inevitably inconsistent. In this area, Mazarin, wrestling with the same problems, with demands constantly exceeding resources, followed the master's example, and with even less care for principle. Richelieu took pains to set out the ideal in his *Testament* and *Maxims*. He also envisaged a healthier tax regime in his proposals to the Notables. Mazarin was entirely the pragmatist and instilled in the young Louis XIV a healthy caution. In some form or another, the five remaining Estates would survive until the Revolution. Mazarin's main concern would be with the *parlements* and their potential for disruption. His approach, as always, was that of the diplomat, working painstakingly through individuals, playing on their needs.

7

Maritime and Commercial Projects

The ruthless autocrat, the pragmatic trimmer: both notions of Richelieu are valid – but insufficient to encompass the whole man and his breadth of vision. After 1635 little was left of his time, or the crown's resources, for maritime and commercial projects. They had been 'eroded by fiscality' (Hauser). The creative planner of early years had been blown off course, but not before he had set out an agenda and taken initiatives important both in themselves and as a precedent for the more sustained and comprehensive labours of Colbert.

His family's seafaring tradition was perhaps the least among several reasons for Richelieu's interest in maritime affairs. Often we see him thinking beyond what was conventional in his age and class. Aware that France was vulnerable in a Europe dominated by Spain, he saw the need to act. Among those who influenced him was Antoine de Montchrétien, a Norman, owner of iron forges, tireless writer and publicist, who examined, in his *Treatise on Political Economy* (1615), economic aspects of the struggle for power. Contemporary debate was stimulated by the growth of oceanic trade, improvements in ship-building, the example of the English and Dutch and, for Frenchmen, the sense of falling behind in a competitive world. Other countries were prospering from trade from which they were excluded; capital and skills were lacking, so foreigners provided goods and service; money was being drained from the kingdom. Writers could point to natural advantages: a long coastline, excellent harbours, ample forests for timber, a seafaring population; yet the merchant fleet remained small, some ships were built in foreign yards, there was virtually no war fleet. When Richelieu ordered an inquiry, his agents exposed alarming facts: a universal shortage of shipwrights, captains, seamen; idle forges, faulty guns; Nantes was silting up, Boulogne decayed; merchant ships were easy prey; there was no permanent fleet in the Atlantic, only 12 galleys in the Mediterranean. France's geography and history, her long land frontiers and proven vulnerability, had made for a continental, military set of mind, with a consequent bias in policy. The wars of the late sixteenth century had stimulated naval development elsewhere; France's civil wars had inhibited it. Social attitudes also counted. Among the propertied classes there was a deep-seated prejudice against trade: the noble risked rank by the rule of *dérogeance*; the bourgeois aspired to 'live nobly' and given the chance to invest productively, he preferred to buy land or office.

Richelieu was a politician to his finger-tips. He showed repeatedly that he could respond flexibly to new dangers, find ways round new obstacles. Often he was harassed by the demands of his lonely position. He did not neglect his own financial interests – indeed he rarely delegated private business in the way that Mazarin would do to Colbert. Through all he maintained an inner life, responsible to art, devout, contemplative. He could think in compartments. Most remarkably he continued to think creatively. His mind kept open house to new ideas. His salon welcomed experts. He liked to work through independent-minded men, like Charnacé, architect of the treaty of Bärwalde. Projects were judged by their relevance to his central concern – for an ordered, prosperous, secure land. At first there were two overriding objectives: protecting commercial interests and thwarting the Spanish war effort. For example, the main aim of his *réglement* of 1625, providing for the construction of ships and defence of harbours, was to protect French Mediterranean merchants against Barbary pirates. A tactical aim throughout was to control the sea passage to Italy so as to force Spanish vessels out to the high seas. Isaac de Razilly was an influential adviser. He appealed to Richelieu's taste for the heroic. His message was simple. Poor nobles should be encouraged to take to the sea. The state should foster the formation of companies for overseas trade and settlement. The navy should be strong enough to protect French merchants against foreign pirates.

A precondition of naval expansion was reform of the traditional system of control. The admiral of France was a feudal dignitary and a soldier. The admiralties of Guyenne and Brittany, vested in the governor, were further obstructions to reform. Richelieu's actions here reveal much about the times, his own philosophy and methods. Admiral Montmorency had made a start, when he unified the Admiralty of France with those of Guyenne and Brittany. In 1626 Richelieu bought the office, abolished it and transferred its powers to himself, as *Grand Maître et Surintendant-général du Commerce*. The office gave him control both of merchant shipping and of the royal navy that he planned to create. A tussle with the *parlement* of Brittany was resolved when Vendôme was made to give up his governorship in Richelieu's favour; his complicity in the Chalais plot was convenient. When Guise, another governor of suspect loyalty, was ousted from Provence in 1630, the crown's control of the coastline was complete. Meanwhile La Rochelle had fallen and Richelieu had been adding steadily to his strategic holding of governorships (including La Rochelle) and other commands, and to his personal estates in western France. In this evolving pattern three strands are distinct but interwoven: his personal aggrandisement, his search for security in the form of a provincial network of command, revenue and patronage – and the interests of the state. He was well rewarded. After ten years the known revenues of the *Grand Maître* were over 200,000 *livres* a year. The state was also well served.

The instructions to deputies of the Third Estate in 1614 had voiced merchants' concerns. The Assembly of Notables was used to launch a wide-ranging programme of action. In January 1627 Richelieu addressed them himself. His proposals reveal more about his philosophy of government and view of society than his *Testament politique*, where art took a hand and he wrote (and others wrote for him) with an eye to posterity. He took a broad view of the country's needs. His proposals were both traditional and innovative. The imposition of order through special assises, reduction of the *taille*, the redemption of royal demesne land, were familiar aspirations and remedies. Reduction of the number of schools teaching the liberal arts, provision of education for technical pursuits, the training of certain *sages gentilshommes* in state affairs, relaxation of the rules of *dérogeance* – here are glimpses into an idea of a society that anticipates, as it influenced, the work of Colbert.

To interest the Notables was the easiest part. Rhetoric, principles, plans: the dawn was bright. What did the day bring? Inevitably the achievement was patchy. The naval strategy was sound, reflecting the benefits of central control. Ships were concentrated in a few ports, notably Brest and Le Havre. Each was given overseers for maintenance, building and defence. All were placed under the direction of Richelieu's uncle, Amador de la Porte, designated *intendant-général*. Richelieu rarely let vital business pass out of the hands of his small circle of relations and clients. Amid constant disappointments, in 1638–9, he was gratified by the victories of his wayward nephew, Pontcourlay, commander of galleys in the Mediterranean.

For recruitment Richelieu adopted the idea of a register of captains, but it was never properly used. By 1635 three squadrons were operating in the Atlantic, one, beside the galleys, in the Mediterranean: 46 sail in all. He had to import some foreign shipwrights, even buy foreign ships since French ships tended to be faulty in design and construction. He did not achieve anything approaching parity with the Dutch, English or Spanish. The mainly smaller French ships, around 300 tons, were better suited to raiding than to set battles. The achievement only appears considerable when set against the initial weakness and the increasing concentration of resources on the army, and related to the trading and colonial enterprises which it was designed to protect.

Richelieu appreciated the importance of colonies. He surveyed the record of early ventures, failed companies and stranded settlers and resolved to give new merchant companies sufficient rights to make them viable. The parochialism of Breton and Norman towns and their resentment at special privileges, helped destroy the first company, that of Morbihan. The names of companies changed, there were new groupings, but the principle remained the same: a guaranteed monopoly and special inducements. The name of one company, *La Nouvelle France* (1628), directed by Razilly, indicates its specific purpose. To the economic arguments for a little France overseas, Father Joseph added that of missionary opportunity. Samuel Champlain, pioneer explorer and colonist, claimed that the salvation of one soul was worth more than the conquest of an empire. Capucins, Jesuits, Ursuline nuns and Hospitalières contributed glorious pages to the record of Christian evangelism. Less impressive, at first sight, was that of the fur traders and soldiers. A setback was the loss of Quebec to the English. Recovered by treaty in 1632 it became the base for ambitious exploration, but it remained tiny. By 1643 there were only 300 Frenchmen in Canada. Richelieu had envisaged 4,000. When, 20 years later, Colbert sent Jean Talon out to develop it, there were about 2,500.

A fragile enterprise had survived. It could grow. It was part of a wider movement. Colonists were going out to the West Indies in sponsored groups. Mazarin showed little interest in colonies or in the navy and it was left to Colbert to return to Richelieu's ideal. Colbert's colonies were to be replicas of France, Catholic, seigneurial, authoritarian, directed from home. The future would show that there was to be vitality in a different form, that of the English colonies, accidental rather than designed, growing with adventurers or religious exiles, and at first left to fend for themselves. Yet, if Wolfe had lost the battle of Quebec, the outcome of a century's rivalry, the end of New France would not have served to reinforce conventional judgements about its principles. Richelieu's paternalist approach, idealist in sympathies but practical in aims and methods, had provided the impetus for a heroic enterprise.

Richelieu could always change his mind if the evidence convinced him. Like Olivarez, concerned about imports and imbalance of trade, he put his faith in sumptuary laws to discourage spending on luxuries: only nobles were to wear silk, for example; the ownership of carriages was discouraged. Persuaded by the example of Marseilles and its Provençal hinterland that import trade could also stimulate exports and, therefore, native manufactures, he began to plan for the furtherance of Mediterranean trade. As ever there were no half measures. His confidential envoy on several missions, des Hayes de Courmenin, was sent to see the Tsar, to negotiate an alternative route for Persian trade. Hauser's famous attribution of a 'Grand Design' to Richelieu's commercial policy is perhaps grander than this and other ventures deserve. There were rewards, however, for imaginative and – at least by proxy – venturesome initiatives: a commercial treaty with the Tsar and a reduction in the Danish tolls that had discouraged the French from venturing into the Baltic.

There was, moreover, a discernible strategy which becomes evident when the whole record is assessed. He commissioned the Baron de Beausoleil to survey mines. One development important for the future was the promotion of sugar refining. Like Sully before him Richelieu realised the importance of communications and transport by land and water and the engineering that made improvements possible. In 1642 the vital Briaire canal joining the Seine and Loire rivers, started in 1610, was opened. Most road and river tolls were reduced. A royal postal service was established. With it society gained an efficient service; the government, typically, a new range of offices for sale. Immediate financial needs were always a factor. But there was planning for the longer term. Richelieu anticipated Colbert in fostering the growth of native manufactures. A glass industry was founded. Textiles mattered most: in his *Testament* he enthused about the quality of the products of Touraine, the plush, taffeta, silk and velvet, all the best in the world. The propietorial pride of a Frenchman for his land is a side of Richelieu that deserves notice. Sully, Richelieu, Colbert: on the basis of their ideas and actions it would be possible to write about the continuity of 'mercantilist' policies, at least up until the 1680s. It is a sequence in which the name of Mazarin is notably absent.

8

Church and State

Priest and politician: at once there is a presumption of strain, if not conflict, in the double role. A feature of recent research about Richelieu's career has been the emphasis on the mundane, his power-broking, his fortune-making. Remarkably there remains intact, even further illuminated, the picture of the other Richelieu, the precocious bishop remaining the conscientious priest who found time, between 1636 and 1639, to compose his *Treatise of Christian Perfection*, in which he advocated the mystical goal of the presence of God. He grew up, and his career developed, in the intense world of the *dévôts*. An early influence was that of Pierre Bérulle, founder of the Oratory, designed to establish a new way of spiritual life and model for the priesthood. Bérulle looked to the young Richelieu to promote his cause. Richelieu's anti-Habsburg policy appears to have caused a decisive break with Bérulle and his political ally, Marillac. He did not, however, cease to be *dévôt* in spirit and work for the church. Vincent de Paul, pioneering and directing charitable efforts, had his ear: it was Richelieu who asked the founder of the *Dames de la Charité* and the Lazarists to take up the training of priests.

Accumulating benefices, gaining control, where possible, of the religious orders, increasingly influential in the appointment of bishops, Richelieu was indeed concentrating power in his own hands. He was careful, for example, to guard his position

38

at the vulnerable point where the king's conscience might be touched, by securing the appointment of his brother, Alphonse, to be Grand Almoner (1632) in place of the Cardinal de la Rochefoucauld, scrupulous and severe. The reforming process was part of a larger political design. One disappointed client, who had hoped for a bishopric, became his fiercest critic. For Matthieu de Morgues, Richelieu was a consummate hypocrite who used the church, and religious claims, for his own ends. It was not the predominant view. The visitor of the Carmelites reported favourably to Rome on the use Richelieu made of his position. He could justly say that he acquired such key posts as abbot of Cîteaux, and Cluny, in order to influence the direction of reform.

Bergin has shown that the effect of Richelieu's influence over episcopal appointments, besides extending his *clientèle*, and consolidating his influence in western France, was markedly to raise the standard: those with pastoral gifts might expect promotion; experience weighed more than aristocratic influence; relatively few came from the older nobility. In appointments that reflected Richelieu's efforts to reform the theology faculty of the University of Paris, theologians were preferred to lawyers. Slackness in a bishop brought sharp rebuke. He even asked the Pope (1638) to authorise a commission of French bishops to investigate such cases. The disciplinary aspect – the church as an instrument of control – should be stressed. It can be seen in his persisting interest in the Huguenot question, where he hoped for conversions through reasonable argument and good example; also, however, in another mood, in his fierce reaction to the case of Urbain Grandier, canon of Loudun, eventually burned (1634) after charges of sorcery had been investigated by his agent, Laubardemont. The case of Grandier was specially sensitive as it represented the *dérèglement* that was the very opposite to the main tenets of his political philosophy – and that on his home ground of Poitou! Again there were political implications in the case of the abbé Saint-Cyran, whom he imprisoned (1638) without, however, stifling the Jansenism which posed problems for his successor. Was it Saint-Cyran's extremism, his known relationship with Jansen, Flemish apologist for Spain, or the potentially dangerous links with *parlementaires* that had most worried Richelieu?

Special cases aside, the lasting impression is of a spiritual vocation, devout life and reforming purpose. It is revealed in his relationship with Father Joseph. Fellow Poitevin, nobleman, Capuchin friar, Richelieu's friend, confidant, spiritual adviser and personal envoy on diplomatic missions, Father Joseph was an enigma in his time – and is still. The self-torturing ascetic much engaged in worldly business; the enthusiast for crusade against the Turks who claimed that its precondition was the defeat of Spain – was he a better Frenchman than Catholic? Father Joseph, one of nature's fanatics, complements Richelieu, the more gracious, subtler man. Undoubtedly Richelieu leaned on the friar for moral support, sympathy and inspiration. He may have envisaged him as his successor. Father Joseph's death, in 1638, left a gap that no one else could fill.

A continuing source of tension throughout the period was Gallicanism. Richelieu, like Mazarin, had to cope with the tension arising from opposed and, for some, irreconcileable views of ecclesiastical authority: the Roman, or 'ultramontane', comprehensive and absolute; and that of many Gallicans in *Parlement*, and some bishops: that the king should be master in all secular aspects, the Pope's authority being confined to matters of doctrine. In 1614 the Gallican question produced the fiercest debate in the States-General. Richerism, named after Edmond Richer, who believed that 'bishops are an essential part of the church and the pope is an accessory', was a further disruptive force. Typically, Richelieu engaged him in private debate and gained a modification of his views. He could not so easily deal with the ultramontane *dévôts*, offended by his alliances with Protestant states. Gaston of Orléans' marriage to Marguerite of Lorraine (1632) raised a sensitive strategic question. Working to nullify the marriage – invalid, it was claimed, because not sanctioned by the king – and using his brother, Alphonse, now cardinal archbishop of Lyons, to handle the case in Rome, Richelieu was in his diplomatic element. It was convenient to him to use the threat of schism to bring diplomatic pressure on Rome – a precedent of which Louis XIV would be aware. Richelieu may even have been tempted to widen the base of his support by appealing to Gallican prejudices, particularly against the Jesuits, ever vulnerable to the charge that they advocated tyrannicide. On balance, however, Richelieu seems to have inclined to the moderation expressed by Pierre de Marca, in a book dedicated to him (1641), arguing for equilibrium between the primacy of Rome and the requirements of the civil power.

In 1643 Mazarin ordered Saint-Cyran's release. As in other fields of policy a gentler style is indicated. The fiery Basque died; Jansenism did not. Dealing with it, Mazarin reveals aspects of his religious temperament, quite different from Richelieu's. He was little interested in theology, unresponsive apparently to the spiritual ardour which found expression in Jansenism. His was a secular approach, the papal diplomat's, judging issues by political criteria. He was never ordained priest. He displayed the amiable face of Christian faith, unquestioning, humane, displayed in gentle manners and generous actions, and latterly, when he was ill, in striking fortitude. He was from the start suspect to *dévôts*. He dealt with church matters against the background of hostility and scorn that was eventually to colour opposition during the *Fronde*. The *conseil de conscience* which started to meet regularly during the Regency, was dominated by his critics; yet he used it to display his credentials as cardinal, and concern (for all his own unblushing pluralism) for sound appointments. He kept the confidence of the pious queen; he influenced his godson, the young Louis, to take seriously his religious duties. He won back Vincent de Paul, who had been his severe critic. In September 1652, only months after urging Mazarin's dismissal, he wrote: 'Mazarin's only ambition is for the good of the king, the queen and the state'. It is interesting how many came to Mazarin to criticise, stayed to talk and went off to praise. When *dévôts* posed the greatest political risk, in *frondeur* Paris, he was fortunate in the unsatisfactory character of their leading representative. Shifty and shamelessly promiscuous, Paul de Gondi, *co-adjuteur* to his uncle, the archbishop of Paris, later archbishop himself (better known to posterity as the Cardinal de Retz and as author of entertaining memoirs) could give no moral leadership.

Richelieu saw in Jansen the Flemish apologist for Spain; Mazarin saw in his followers, most obviously in their spiritual centre, Port Royal, the links with suspect *parlementaires*. Antoine Arnauld's obstinacy, in defending the position defined in his book *De la fréquente communion* (1643) and Pascal's subsequent attack on the Jesuits in the *Lettres provinciales* (1656), were too close, in time and personal associations, to the *Fronde*. Louis XIV would inherit Mazarin's prejudice and follow

41

the minister's relatively hard line, without his saving caution, or the humour which had enabled Mazarin to savour Pascal's wit and style. As ever Mazarin had to take diplomatic factors into account. By condemning the Five Propositions (extracted from Jansen's study of Saint Augustine) Pope Innocent X had, in effect, declared Jansenism heretical (1653). After that, though he was concerned to contain rather than to inflame, Mazarin did not dare let his enemies, in Rome or in Paris, portray him as anything but a good Catholic.

At the same time he knew that *parlementaire* Gallicans would bristle. Indeed *Parlement* refused to register the Pope's bull and a *lit de justice* was required. Mazarin's resolve was stiffened by the behaviour of Retz. When he escaped from prison, *curés* supporting Port Royal had infuriated ministers by causing the *Te Deum* to be sung. They would not know that he had written to Anne offering his help 'to exterminate Jansenism'. His confidence growing, Mazarin closed the Jansenist schools and secured a redrafting of the face-saving theological formula. It would continue to trouble scrupulous Jansenist consciences. It can, however, be held that the 'Peace of the Church' negotiated (1668) by archbishop Péréfixe, on the basis of a revised formula which the Port Royal nuns could sign, represented Mazarin's thinking more accurately than the stern words and measures of an ailing man; certainly more than the persecution of later years, when Louis XIV would rouse just that temper of opposition in *Parlement* that Mazarin would have been most anxious to avoid.

9

Art as Propaganda

For both cardinals art was important for itself and for the purposes it served. From his first involvement with Marie de Médicis, herself a lavish and purposeful patron, Richelieu followed in the Italian tradition, adopted by the French – as notably in the Fontainebleau of Francis I – of commissioned art in palatial settings to advertise the might of the sovereign and the benefits of his civilising rule. The devices of classical humanism, in art as in literature meant to improve and impress, were exploited to manipulate the contemporary mind. In Paris, in the Palais Cardinal, using Marie's architect Le Mercier, and her artists, notably Poussin, Vouet and Champaigne; in his grand new château at Richelieu, and at Rueil, the relatively modest country retreat outside Paris where he was most at ease (and able, it seems, to enjoy its superb gardens) Richelieu's client architects and artists worked to his instructions and within the constraints of a total plan.

As in his patronage of letters, 'protection' signified explicitly that an artist was his *créature*. The visitor to his galleries was given the *patron*'s lesson in history. He would see Philippe de Champaigne's portrait of the cardinal at the end of a line of the great figures of French history. The painters were rarely free agents. Accepting the cardinal's fee, they furthered his propaganda. In the symbolism of the Galérie des Hommes Illustres, for example, could be read: loyalty to the king, fidelity to the

43

church, respect for the great families of France, defence against the foreigner, willingness to give one's life in the service of France. In the gallery at Richelieu, where also his new town was intended to be an administrative centre (almost, could one say, an alternative court?) no fewer than 51 paintings celebrated the achievements of the cardinal. 'In a complex, mutually supportive interplay, the ambitious images of Richelieu and French preeminence fed upon each other, leaving an enduring example of vigorous state *dirigisme* in French cultural affairs' (Caldecott).

It is arguable that Richelieu's interest and involvement in theatre, music and dance reflected more of his personal taste and interest, the human face behind the heroic image, self-dramatising but sincere. He enjoyed the world of theatre and helped make it respectable. The theatre in the Palais Cardinal was designed to be the best equipped in the world. He suggested plots and collaborated in writing several plays. Conversant with the current debates between the 'Ancients' and the 'Moderns', he would intervene when he thought that a play offended against accepted rules or the conventions that he favoured. It was probably at his instigation that critics forced Corneille to revise *Le Cid* (1637). He might appreciate a performance for itself, but a subsidised theatre had to serve the regime. Desmarets' *L'Europe* (1641) as a weighty celebration of France's pre-eminence. A court ballet of the same year, *De la prosperité des armes de la France*, marked his union, through his niece's marriage, to the Condé family and the blood royal.

The range of Richelieu's interests, the scale of the activity, are breathtaking. The way in which separate enterprises could serve a single grand design and the patron's distinctive elevating idea of France is revealed in an institution which, holding a guardian's brief over the language, has remained influential to this day. The *Académie française* (1635) was not conceived simply to be the arbiter of taste in language. Contemporaries realised that. *Parlement* was sufficiently wary to delay, for two years, registration of its letters patent. Richelieu took Valentine Conrat's *salon*, intended to be a place of escape from official business and for the meeting of cultivated minds, and grafted on to it his conception of a body committed to promoting the image and interests of France. Through his agent Boisrobert he influenced elections to secure a majority of those who would write his script. Two, Servien and Séguier, were ministers of state.

Several members of Conrat's *salon* who served Richelieu's opponents were reluctant to join the new body. They were told that the cardinal was 'not used to meeting resistance' and warned that the society might be dissolved. Whether they were bullied, flattered, recruited or rejected, it is no wonder that some of his foremost contemporaries were over-awed by this most exacting of patrons, that some loathed him – or that some modern Frenchmen revere his memory. The Academy's seal bears his effigy.

Another private venture which became, under Richelieu's direction, an instrument of propaganda was the *Gazette*, initially edited by Théophraste Renaudot. *Le Mercure françois* already existed, under the editorship of Father Joseph, but it only appeared once a year. In return for a monopoly of news, Renaudot, another Poitevin, ensured that his weekly reporting would be favourable to the régime. 'The *Gazette* shall play its part', Richelieu wrote, 'or Renaudot will lose his pension'. The cardinal monitored the journal through such trusted agents as Father Joseph and Chavigny, ensured that setbacks would be glossed over and victories puffed up, and used it to promote cherished causes, such as the colonisation of Canada. Alongside the war against Spain, another war was being waged, for the minds and souls of educated French men and women. If the *Fronde* was to show that it was far from won, that hardly detracts from the magnitude of his achievement. Few men, through such varied means, so concerted an effort, have affected so powerfully the political outlook of an age. He saw the way the current was flowing; he showed how it could be canalised and controlled.

In more substantial works, two distinct lines of propaganda can be seen, sometimes in the same book. There were *pièces d'occasion*. In 1632, for example, Cassan wrote arguing that antiquity did not weaken rights but actually strengthened them. His championing of French claims to the Rhineland going back to king Dagobert reflected current concerns about Swedish ambitions. Like many others Cassan's book was dedicated to the cardinal. A loftier essay in political theory, Guez de Balzac's 'Prince' (1631), adapted Machiavelli to the needs of the time and the ideals of the minister with a fresh statement of the morality of the state.

Richelieu wished to impress contemporaries. His *Mémoires*

and Testament Politique show that he also thought much of the verdict of posterity. Conceived, if not actually written by Richelieu, being an account of his rise to power and early ministerial years, the *Mémoires* comprised documents, letters and supporting material: as the reader looks beyond the events and arguments, he may see a coherent philosophy of government: prominent features are the king's Divine Right, his need of a powerful first minister, and, permeating all, the ideal of Christian justice for states as for individuals. In the *Testament*, addressed to Louis XIII, we hear more of the cardinal's voice, as he records his political experience and offers guidance for the future. If a single word can convey what he thought the country needed, it is discipline: that which had been lacking in the turbulent past, which must be enforced if the individualistic, factious French people were to enjoy the benefits of an ordered society. '*Dérèglement*', disorderliness, was the great evil, be it in rebellious nobleman, obstructive *parlementaire* or corrupt finance officer. It is a tribute to Richelieu that some of the best minds of the century, Pascal and Bossuet, for example, would endorse his view.

In 1635 Richelieu, himself steeped in Italian culture, offered to make Mazarin *surintendant de ses collections*. He refused – but did oversee the despatch from Italy of crates of classical sculptures to embellish Richelieu's galleries. In power, predictably, Mazarin devoted much of his time and money to collecting on his own account. The first impression is of continuity, only with a new focus for the same message. But there is a difference, greater than the new patron's preferring the Italian painter of the past to the French painter of the present. The scale was still gigantic: 471 pictures featured in the inventory of the Palais Mazarin. There was less interest in iconography, less intention to convey the lessons of history, but more, in the Roman tradition, of mythology. Mazarin can seem at times more of a dealer than a connoisseur, collecting paintings as he collected jewels and furniture, increasingly, greedily, indiscriminate in his later years. By contrast, Richelieu's conception of the role of art, as that of literature, was unique in range and ambition: his was a total policy, grandiose and inimitable. He sought to win contemporary minds and to ensure his future fame.

With his taste for the sumptuous and decorative, and his special love for the ephemeral art of the ballet and for the devices employed to produce spectacular effects, Mazarin may seem to have been more purposeful than Richelieu, more self-indulgent in patronage. Inevitably that patronage faltered during the *Fronde*. The literary world was divided as authors and artists looked for other patrons, notably the munificent Fouquet. Mazarin showed little interest in the use of patronage to encourage the young painter to stay at home. Le Brun, Séguier's protégé, had to wait till 1661 and Colbert's ministry to receive royal commissions. As Mazarin's agent Colbert had learned the importance of such patronage, and of the danger of letting it flow from Retz – or even Fouquet. In 1656 he acted as broker in an approach to the writer Jacques Dupuy, with a lucrative office to encourage him to think of himself as Mazarin's man.

It may be fruitless to try to distinguish between collector, power broker, and lover of art. Even where some political end can be recognised, there is evidence of an interest in art and scholarship for its own sake. Mazarin's great library of some 40,000 volumes, the compilation, under his instructions, of Gabriel Naudé, was designed to be an instrument of learning as much as a demonstration of Mazarin's munificence. Naudé described it as 'the most beautiful, the best and the largest library which has been brought together in the world'. From the start it was a haven for scholars. Its dispersal during the *Fronde* was felt keenly by Mazarin; its restoration was a priority. Everything to do with Mazarin was on the grandest scale. He bequeathed the library to the Collège des Quatre Nations, funded by his legacy and designed to encourage learning and to educate gentlemen from the lands annexed by the great treaties of Westphalia and the Pyrenees. An imaginative educational enterprise serving a significant political end – would not Richelieu have approved?

10

The Struggle for Security

In 1624 the Habsburgs appeared to dominate Europe and Richelieu, therefore, to have a limited range of options. One reflected
the views of the *bons francais* expressed in the propaganda
which he commissioned – but did not allow to constrict his
freedom of choice: to find ways of damaging the Spanish war
machine. One vulnerable section of the 'Spanish road', the vital
line of supply to the Netherlands, was the Val Telline, the
mountain pass linking Lombardy and the Tyrol. It had already
been probed when, in 1622, France, acting with Savoy and
Venice, had secured the removal of Spanish garrisons, but then
agreed to allow Papal garrisons to be installed in their place. For
France too the pass was vital, affording access to her ally Venice.
The expulsion of the Papal force (in which Mazarin was a
captain) and occupation of the valley by French troops (November, 1624) was Richelieu's first aggressive venture. Almost immediately it was compromised by Huguenot risings in France.

Another option was indicated by the need to subdue the
Huguenots and therefore to come to a temporary accom-
modation with Spain. That led to the treaty of Monçon (1626)
which allowed the Spanish freedom of passage through the Val
Telline. The subsequent defensive alliance with Spain left Richelieu free to buttress his domestic position and to deal with the
Huguenots. His allies, the United Provinces, Venice and Savoy,
were outraged.

Eventually a third option had to be considered: the financing of reliable allies to fight in Germany and check the Imperialist advance. Meanwhile England came briefly into Richelieu's calculations, with the marriage of Charles I to Henrietta Maria (1625). Under Buckingham's wilful influence, English policy, first directed against Spain, was erratic. Espousing the cause of the Huguenots of La Rochelle, and provoking a war against France, he gave Richelieu a reason to assault the city. It was exactly what he needed, to show that a good Frenchman could also be a good Catholic and to deflect criticism of other aspects of policy.

In these early years Richelieu seems essentially pragmatic, reacting flexibly to each situation as it arose. Underlying all was his conviction that the Habsburgs thought in supremacist terms, that 'universal sovereignty' was no empty phrase, that the advance of Catholicism meant necessarily the advance of the dynasty, the constriction of France and a threat to its security. Even before the Mantuan Succession crisis, since 1618, when the Bohemian revolt had first brought war to Germany, and the renewal of Spain's war against the United Provinces, there was evidence of the Habsburgs' intention to act in concert, and of their determination to pursue war until their objectives had been achieved. The religious zeal of the Emperor Ferdinand II did not conceal the fact that every Catholic victory in Germany was a potential gain for the family and its influence in Germany. Philip IV's Spain, directed by Olivarez, was still, in mentality, the Spain of Philip II. The Habsburg cause knew no frontiers. The arguments of 50 years back, when Leaguers looked to Spain, and *politiques* to a national interest that transcended religious differences, came alive again in the propaganda of Richelieu's critics – and clients.

So he did not waver in hostility towards the Habsburgs. Briefly, however, it suited him to conceal it, to concentrate on the siege of La Rochelle. Even after its successful conclusion, he was cautious. If he had to attack, it was so as to be seen to be defending France's vital interests, his king's honour. He was keenly aware of France's military weakness and of Habsburg strength, shown by Spinola's capture of Breda (1625), and Wallenstein's and Tilly's victories in 1626. At home, in that year, the Chalais plot (1626) showed him to be vulnerable. Prudence suggested that safety lay in policies that reassured the *dévôts*. He also had a more positive reason for inclining towards peace: it was essential, if the reform programme presented to the Notables were to have any impact.

He could count on the stubborn resistance of the Dutch to avert the worst – the Spanish recovery of the lost provinces in the Netherlands. He was fortunate in his opponents' blunders. In turn Buckingham, Olivarez, the duke of Savoy, the Emperor, provided him with the opportunity – and justification – to counter-attack. Following the death in 1627 of the old Gonzaga duke, Olivarez was drawn by the precipitate action of his general Cordoba to challenge the right of the duc de Nevers to succeed to the duchy of Mantua and marquisate of Montferrat: the lands bordered on Spanish Milan and the fortresses of Mantua and Casale commanded vital areas. When Spanish troops moved to besiege Casale, Richelieu was able to intervene, knowing that Pope Urban VIII would be sympathetic to any move that might check Spain's ambitions in North Italy. Savoy was tempted to support Spain. The Emperor refused to 'invest' Nevers with what, in law, were still Imperial fiefs. Emboldened by the surrender of La Rochelle, Richelieu first invaded and overran Savoy, secured passage to Mantua and sent his troops on to relieve the besieged city (March, 1629).

Since the action only increased the determination of Olivarez to mount a second siege to secure Casale, and persuaded the Emperor that he must send troops to assist, the episode was crucial. If Richelieu had failed then, or later when a second invasion of Savoy led to the capture of the fortress of Pinerolo and securing of his supply line to Italy, his position in council, already under attack, could hardly have been sustained. He had staked everything on the argument, presented in a famous memorandum (April, 1630), that Louis must secure Pinerolo: 'to be master of Italy . . . or forget about Italy for ever'. The choice was his. Richelieu was quite clear in his own mind about the price that had to be paid. As ever, he was careful to ensure that the king too should have no illusions: it would be the king's decision and his commitment. If he chose war he must attack Savoy at once and give up all thoughts of ease and reform at home. That debate, followed by months of delay as the king first decided to invade, then became ill, and while the faction of Marie de Médicis intrigued against the cardinal, was the background to the Day of Dupes and to his confirmation in office, strengthened by the success of the policy he had urged.

For the Emperor the outcome was disastrous. The Habsburgs' ambitious plan to establish a base on the Baltic had already foundered when Wallenstein failed in his siege of Stralsund (1628), but not before the Dutch and Swedes had been made aware of the threat to their commercial and strategic interests. The Emperor's Edict of Restitution (1629), aimed at the return of secularised lands to the church, alienated German princes who might otherwise have preferred to stay neutral, notably Saxony and Brandenburg, and created conditions favourable to Swedish intervention. His diversion of troops to Mantua was therefore, to say the least, untimely. It helped focus the minds of the Electors on the need to make the Emperor dismiss Wallenstein: that was the price the Emperor had to pay for their accepting his son as King of the Romans, with the expectation of succeeding to his throne.

The Habsburgs found themselves over-stretched, therefore, at a time when Richelieu could count on a revulsion of German opinion against the Emperor and also on the military power of Sweden. He repudiated the settlement of the Mantuan question by his envoys at the Diet of Regensburg (1630) because they had accepted a clause debarring him from assisting the Emperor's enemies in Germany. His action could be justified by his success in maintaining his Italian strongholds, notably Pinerolo, and by the Peace of Cherasco (1631), negotiated by Mazarin. France now had the capacity to intervene in Italian affairs. Spain had gained nothing in territory or reputation. The Dutch had a respite. The balance of power in Germany was about to swing in a way which altered dramatically all assumptions about Habsburg power.

Richelieu's Italian policy should be judged in the light of a wider vision and strategy. Germany now became his chief preoccupation. His diplomatic instructions were clear: they were intended to express France's interest without alarming the princes. Urging the dismissal of Wallenstein, restoration of peace in Italy and Spain's evacuation of the Palatinate, he was lending weight to their programme. He knew, however, that Spain would not comply with the last, nor would the Emperor desist from military operations to recover secularised bishoprics

51

(they would lead to the horrifying sack of Magdeburg), unless a new military force was brought to bear. Despite Father Joseph's efforts, the Catholic duke of Bavaria, who had gained an electorate and the Upper Palatinate by supporting the Emperor, would not change his allegiance. Those were the realistic considerations behind Richelieu's negotiations with Gustavus Adolphus, first to extract him from his Polish war, then to secure his military aid. The treaty of Barwälde (January, 1631), backed by a subsidy, was followed by a successful Swedish campaign, Gustavus' victory at Breitenfeld and the transformation of the military and political balance in Germany.

There had always been a risk; now there was a price to pay. Alliance with the heretic was even harder to justify when Gustavus flouted his treaty commitment to respect Catholic property. It was not Richelieu's policy to bring about a Protestant ascendancy but to restore a degree of balance. The Swedish king's death at the battle of Lützen (November, 1632) was therefore less than a catastrophe. His army had not been defeated. The Swedes, with the German Protestant princes' League of Heilbronn, maintained the struggle. Richelieu's main concern was the security of France's eastern frontier. Once again an enemy's move gave him the pretext to act. Gaston of Orléans posed a constant threat to the crown – how serious Richelieu had been reminded during Louis XIII's recent illness and then, in 1632, by his support of Montmorency's rising. His secret marriage to Charles of Lorraine's daughter (1630) could not therefore be accepted. A first French occupation of part of Lorraine in 1632 was not enough to deter duke Charles from cooperating with the Emperor. In September 1633 Louis ordered his troops into Nancy. In 1634 Richelieu started a legal process for the annulment of Gaston's marriage. Charles abdicated in favour of his brother – who soon fled. The French then annexed the duchy.

Between Richelieu and Olivarez there grew suspicions, in Olivarez' case verging on the paranoiac, with a tendency to read aggressive intent into every move: the word 'feud', suggesting the irreconcilable, is, however more appropriate than the 'duel' often used to describe their antagonism. Given Richelieu's reluctance to commit himself to open war, and the opposition in the Spanish council to Olivarez' first war plan of 1634, we may be inclined to see the conflict of Spain and France in terms of irreconcilable interests. So long as Philip IV and his minister held to their main war aim, the subjugation of the Netherlands, and so long as Richelieu was actively seeking ways of buttressing French strength around the eastern frontier, open war remained a likely outcome. Until 1637 and the loss of Breda, victory in the Netherlands looked feasible to Madrid. Only after 1640 and the revolts of Catalonia and Portugal was it plainly out of the question. After so long a struggle, such vast expenditure of blood and treasure, it took time to adjust psychologically to new facts, those which historians see as evidence of 'the decline of Spain'. Meanwhile the Spanish must control the land route from Milan to Brussels. The French threatened it by their continuing presence in North Italy, their subsidies to the Swedes, the occupation of Lorraine and of several Alsatian towns, and the 'protection' of Trier. Such were the probes and bridgeheads that Richelieu had preferred to open war. But war was what many at the French court were now demanding.

Olivarez was heartened by the victory of the joint Imperialist and Spanish army over the Swedes at Nördlingen (1634). Sure that his armies could defeat the French, he was resolved to draw France into war. When the Spanish occupied Trier, and imprisoned the bishop, France's client, Richelieu could no longer resist the arguments of honour and interest. France declared war in May 1635 – on Spain only, though the Austrian Habsburgs were plainly partners in counsel and war. After the Peace of Prague (1635), between the Emperor and the German princes, an end to the German war might have been expected. The main obstacle was the persisting belligerence of Olivarez.

At once events showed that Richelieu had been right to hold back. In 1635 the French army that invaded Flanders dissolved into a disorderly rabble. In 1636 the Habsburg armies struck deep into France. It was to be remembered as 'the year of Corbie': the surrender of that Somme town raised fears about the safety of Paris. Problems of supply and autumn rains counted for more than French resistance in persuading the Habsburg generals to call off the operation. It might have been different if the southern invasion, from Catalonia, had been mounted simultaneously: in the following year, a Spanish force was defeated at Leucate. In 1638, after a further treaty with the Swedes, France declared war on the Emperor.

Ultimate French success thereafter depended chiefly on three conditions: successful cooperation with the Swedish armies, the French operating mainly in and around Alsace, the Swedes in Saxony and the north; the continuing resolution of the Dutch, as they looked to better the terms on which they might expect independence; the exhaustion of the Habsburg powers' resources and will to go on. As war had spread, so more combatants had interests to satisfy, more victims called for compensation. Seventeenth-century warfare was not conducive to quick results: few battles, not Breitenfeld, not Nördlingen, not even Rocroi, were decisive in the sense that they destroyed one side's capacity to fight on. There were difficulties in the supply and control of armies which the German war had shown to be damaging not only to civilian communities, but also to the paymaster states. Richelieu was embarking on a war of attrition, calling for nerve and patience, in the knowledge that the French people would have to pay higher taxes, the state would have to raise more loans and sell more offices. Not only were cherished projects threatened, but the good order and stability of the state.

Once committed, however, Richelieu was in no hurry to make peace – at least one that would bring no significant advantages to France. Whether it be the fall of Breisach (1638), the shattering victory of the Dutch, and sinking of 32 Spanish ships at the battle of the Downs (1639), or the revolts of Catalonia and Portugal that marked the change, it is plain that by 1640 the initiative was passing to France. So new questions arise. Was Richelieu indifferent to the suffering of the French people – demonstrated in popular revolts? Or was he well aware of the human and material cost of pursuing the war course, but convinced that it was both necessary and right? Of their nature such questions are unanswerable. There is a strong case, however, based as much on the whole tenor of his career as on the memoranda and instructions in which he expressed his ideas, for arguing that he was sincere in his desire for peace but that he also believed that it must be a lasting peace. Running like a refrain through all his diplomatic instructions is the phrase *'une bonne paix'*. That meant a settlement which would be good for France, for Germany, indeed for all Christendom. It entailed securing for France sufficient lands and bases to offer to the German states a countering weight and influence to that of the Habsburgs, and to serve as warning to the Habsburgs against renewing war. Meanwhile the only convincing arguments would be those of battles lost and armies disintegrating. All pointed to the pursuit of war *à l'outrance*.

On paper, according to official estimates, the nine French armies in the field in 1635 comprised 160,000 men. According to the more reliable estimates of the *commissaires* responsible for musters, around 70,000 men were actually available for campaigns. For that number the money available was still insufficient. Seeing the fortunes being made by contractors and financiers, not least by his *surintendant*, Bullion, Richelieu tended to blame the system. It could not, however, be reformed without a period of peace; in wartime its faults were compounded. From 1635 the government was living hand to mouth, as interest payments swallowed up much of the yield of taxes, and policy was reduced to an increasingly desperate attempt to satisfy creditors and persuade them to pay more – inevitably at higher interest rates.

'The grief of Fuentarabia is killing me': so Richelieu wrote after a siege in 1638 had ended in humiliating rout. His opponent suffered even more. After the French capture of Perpignan in 1642 Olivarez threatened to throw himself out of a window. His Imperial ally was now suffering under the hammer blows of Torstensson and was being offered the chance to negotiate for peace. Not surprisingly, historians have tended to assume that the French had effectively won their war. Though Richelieu would not live to hear of Rocroi, the crowning victory, the long subsequent delays in making peace were due to the complications of treaty-making rather than to any continuing strength in the Habsburg war effort. Yet, up to 1643, the alteration in the military balance is marked more by Habsburg misfortunes, the destruction of the main Spanish fleet by the Dutch at the battle of the Downs (1639), the revolts of Catalans and Portuguese in 1640, than by outright French achievements. The capture of Breisach (1638) was the work of Richelieu's ally, Bernard of Saxe-Weimar. If Richelieu became increasingly unreceptive to Habsburg overtures for peace, it was more because he still believed that his enemies would come off worst in a war of attrition than because he had reason to put his trust in French soldiers. He liked to say that the French were not a military nation. It is truer to say that they had not been schooled to exploit their military potential.

The French army was poorly prepared for war in 1635. Its

problems were no less acute in 1643. In that year Michel Le Tellier became war minister. Between then and 1691 administration of the army was in his hands, then his son's. Not till the personal reign of Louis XIV, and some peacetime years (1661–7), could radical reforms be attempted: essentially these were concerned with recruitment, pay, discipline, training and supply; in sum, the creation of a much larger force, up to a quarter of a million by the 1680s. It was then a regular army in the modern sense, and truly royal in that there was a hierarchy of appointment and command reaching directly to the king. The Le Telliers' reforms highlight the serious weaknesses which constantly frustrated the cardinals, and which Richelieu, in particular, failed to remedy.

All governments maintained armies through some kind of compromise between private enterprise and state control. Though always insufficient, the flow of bullion from America, together with the possession of rich recruiting grounds in Castile and Italy, had enabled Spain to maintain forces on a regular basis. Even so, mutinies were a regular feature as troops used their bargaining power to secure their pay. In Germany, a contracting general was expected to maintain his troops through the 'contributions' levied on the civilian population. To keep him loyal, lands and titles were offered. The military entrepreneur, most notably Wallenstein, was thus set on the road to independent sovereignty. That, in a minor way, was the problem posed to Richelieu by Bernard of Saxe-Weimar, who wanted Alsace – but died so conveniently after the fall of Breisach. Special circumstances had long influenced the French approach to the problems of supply and control. After years of civil war it was an axiom with ministers that commanders should not become German-style entrepreneurs. There was, however, a constant demand from nobles for military commissions. Those who received them could expect neither salaries nor independence. Volunteers, still feudal in outlook, they served if and when they pleased. When cash did arrive, they were tempted to defraud government through false claims. There was a high level of absenteeism among officers, little systematic training; no wonder their soldiers deserted in droves. This was the background to the use by government of *intendants* to supervise commanders, often ineffectively. Le Tellier had had that experience. He knew all too well how ineffective civilian control had been when, in 1651, he described the French army as 'a republic, whose cantons are made up of the forces of the corps commanders'. From such anarchy it was a short step for Turenne and Condé to lead their armies on the road to rebellion.

Only ten infantry regiments and some twenty cavalry companies were maintained on a regular basis. Officer appointments were shared between the king and the colonel-general – since 1584 the duc d'Épernon. The rest of the army, expanded in wartime, was raised and officered by the nobility: inevitably the crown was dependent on the goodwill of its more important subjects and on the size of their noble *clientèles*. Crucially important therefore was the crown's relationship with its provincial governors. Richelieu's policy of removing suspect governors and promoting those who were loyal was motivated by more than concern for good order: the war effort depended on it. Without any effective civil administration, with *intendants de l'armeé* limited to a supervisory role, he had no alternative but to rely on the loyalty and ambition of great nobles. They might use their social credit and financial resources in the service of the king; they expected to gain prestige and influence through the growth of their *clientèles*. The whole process, both financing and controlling, was one of bargaining, while the relationship between crown and commanders was one of continuous tension. A general can seem like a broker. When Harcourt reported the fall of Turin (1640) he added a list of promotions and favours required for his officers.

So we see Richelieu pursuing two parallel policies, more readily distinguishable perhaps by the historian than they would have been by him. He sought to build a personal base, with governorships and revenues sufficient to give leverage, and at the same to elevate the reputation of the king, his *gloire*, as a way of strengthening the crown's hold over its generals. His choice of commanders was limited. To ensure loyalty he promoted from within the family or his wider clientage: those chosen were not always the most talented. The Huguenot, La Force, and, his cousin's husband, La Valette, were two who performed indifferently; the duc d'Elbeuf, debarred like other members of the Guise family, would become a *frondeur*. It was fortunate that one family which he took pains to bind to his – that of Condé – prduced, in the young victor of Rocroi, one of the outstanding soldiers of the age.

11

Mazarin and the *Fronde*

The successive episodes known collectively as the *Fronde* developed out of an accumulation of discontents; its causes lay as much in the policies of Richelieu as in the tactics of Mazarin. Richelieu might, however, have found ways of avoiding some of the provocation that led to the crisis of 1648. It arose from pressures felt by particular groups to be intolerable: *parlementaires* and other members of sovereign courts, holders of financial office, and *rentiers*. With old feuds and rivalries, notably that between Vendôme and Condé, and new opportunities afforded by a royal minority, great nobles became involved. Motives were as various as the personalities involved. In general the *frondeurs* were not so much reacting against the growth of royal government as seeking to share in it and benefit from it. In this attitude, along with the lack of any unifying ideology of resistance, lies the reason for the ultimate triumph of the crown. The *Fronde* became, essentially, a struggle for the control of the state. As first minister, Mazarin was, throughout, the embattled central figure. His actions, both before and during the *Fronde*, highlight ways in which he differed from Richelieu as much as similarities in aims and principles. For his career and for the future direction of monarchy, the *Fronde* was crucial. That he survived, and that monarchy emerged in some respects stronger from the ordeal, can be attributed to the ineptitude of his opponents. It also suggests exceptional political skills on his part.

The direct involvement of *intendants* in the collection of the *taille* did not prevent a steady worsening of the financial position between 1643 and 1648. Some provinces had already defaulted in tax payments. In 1639 the *receveur-général* of Champagne complained that he had received nothing that year. After 1643 arrears piled up. Mazarin was mainly interested in the peace negotiations, painfully prolonged by the concern of each participant to gain last-minute advantage. He appointed Particelli d'Hémery, an astute negotiator, with an *intendant*'s experience behind him, to be *surintendant*, and was content – until 1648 when he bowed to the storm and sacrificed him – to leave him to find ways of raising the money for the continuance of war. In that Hémery was successful. He had good contacts and knew where to go for loans. With real income from taxation static or falling, to pay ever rising rates of interest and to persuade *traitants* to continue to lend, he had to devise new taxes. The alternative was bankruptcy.

It was the very ingenuity of Hémery's schemes that caused such political damage. The *toisé* – fining those who had built in Paris since a sixteenth-century ordinance banning such building – was indisputably legal. *Parlement* had, however, a justifiable grievance when the crown ordained that disputes arising from the *toisé* should be decided not by its courts but by the council. As the government tightened its squeeze on office-holders and *rentiers*, cutting salaries and witholding interest payments, with Paris swollen by refugees and afflicted by high bread prices, *parlementaires* sensed that they were moving towards being champions of the people. At a *lit de justice* in September 1645, Anne dropped the *toisé*, but only as part of a package containing several new taxes. Magistrates avowed that their consciences would not allow them to register edicts which they had not examined. Séguier's answer is significant: there were two sorts of conscience, one for private matters, the other for matters of state. For him, as for Mazarin, government was about forces and resources: advances and retreats were ordered in the light of estimates of opponents' strength. Certain leaders of *Parlement*, like president Barillon, who had offended at the outset by warning Anne not to delegate her power to a single minister, were coming to be seen as the enemy. His death in prison in 1645 provided the *Fronde* with its first martyr.

Mazarin's preferred method was to deal with individuals, to suggest where personal advantage lay; together with his pleasant manner it made him seem more like a manipulator than a manager. It aroused uneasiness especially when contrasted with the haughty tone of court and ministerial pronouncements. His fine compliments – 'Fathers of the Fatherland', 'Restorers of France' – were taken by *parlementaires* for signs of weakness. When placatory gestures were made, like the offer of the status of 'perfect nobility', made to members of some provincial sovereign courts and to *trésoriers*, they looked cynical. Meaning to exploit differences of status, ministers contrived only to provoke a more united and resolute opposition.

The prolonged tussle between crown and *Parlement* had some aspects of theatre, with an underlying sense among participants of common interest in the preservation of a system that brought handsome rewards. After a year of argument, in September 1647, *Parlement* registered the decree imposing a tariff on goods entering the city, with the reservation that it was only to last for two years. So they safeguarded their right of registration and asserted the principle that such taxes were a wartime expedient. Mazarin blundered when he issued a new decree annulling that registered by *Parlement* and decree and retained the tax. The people, alerted to the question by *parlementaires*, were now invited to choose between two pronouncements on the same tax: two interpretations of sovereign authority. There is always danger in a precise defining of powers that might otherwise be assumed. Now Mazarin was inviting the worst interpretation of arbitrary power. To compound error he allowed Hémery to proceed with the creation of new offices of *maîtres des réquêtes* and to use a further *lit de justice* to enforce its registration. Just as the future of the *maîtres* as *intendants* was in question, when he had most to gain by keeping their support, Mazarin antagonised them. So they looked to *Parlement* for support. Meanwhile the financial officers, *trésoriers* and *élus*, who had lost ground to the *intendants*, had formed syndicates to defend their interests. If ministers had set out to enlarge and unite the opposition, they could hardly have done better.

If, in August 1648, Mazarin's career had come to an end with the barricades and the first popular and violent defiance of royal authority; if, as he feared, his had been the fate of Concini, his place in history would surely have been that of an adventurer and gambler, who lost through his handling of domestic affairs the credit he might have won for his diplomacy. The Regent Anne's support certainly brought embarrassments: her autocratic temper tended to rouse rather than subdue the spirit of *parlementaire* leaders. But without her support he would have been isolated in the face of virulent hostility. Some of it was inevitable, some surely his fault. Neither Omer Talon, *avocat-général* and therefore representative of the crown in *Parlement*, nor Mathieu Molé, *premier président*, was a radical. The rhetoric of the one, the political tactics of the other, were traditional in emphasis. In particular, Molé was a staunch royalist, determined to recall monarchy to a sense of responsibility for the public good. The actions of the crown drove them to adopt a position of defiance to secure what they held to be a sound constitutional position and to prevent the hotheads, like the veteran magistrate Pierre Broussel, rousing the populace and creating conditions which trouble-makers could exploit.

Beside fiscal novelties and infringement of the rights of office-holders and *rentiers*, *Parlement*'s main concerns were excessive use of the *lit de justice*, arbitrary imprisonment, the diversion of justice from the proper courts to ad hoc commissions or, more regularly, to the royal council, and the excessive powers of the *intendants*. Its programme entailed nothing less than the dismantling of the whole system of war finance at a critical phase – the last phase, Mazarin hoped – of the war. To secure the flow of taxes and loans, he knew that he had to hold on to the political high ground secured by Richelieu. However by 1648, financial and constitutional questions were interweaving to create a new political situation. *Traitants* withheld their advances and the war effort was throttled. In Mazarin's judgement a bold attack was needed. So, in the *lit de justice* of January, *Parlement* was required to accept the Paris tariff, the sale of new offices, a fee on non-feudal property acquired by nobles, and a clutch of new taxes. His big stick was the threat to delay the renewal of the *paulette*.

The crown's theory was that edicts were verified at the *lit*, before examination by the sovereign courts, simply by virtue of their having been read in the presence of the king. For Talon that was 'a kind of illusion in morality and contradiction in politics'. *Parlement* leaders deferred to the king's right but went on to create a climate of protest. Grievances were aired and royal business obstructed. The crown was faced by a united front. The course of the *Fronde* would show that interests were disparate, with most *parlementaires* standing to lose more by opposition to the crown than by cooperation. Painfully, Mazarin would learn to divide and conquer. Meanwhile he and Anne had created the essential preconditions for revolt.

Mazarin thought that Molé put the interests of *Parlement* before those of the crown; Molé thought that they should be identical: both views were put to the test in May 1648, when *Parlement* issued an *arrêt d'union*. In the limited sense in which the *Fronde* can be called a revolution, this was the revolutionary conjuncture. The crown's tactics had assumed that *Parlement* would never ally itself with the other sovereign courts. As Séguier saw, the decision to convene a new body was 'dangerous and prejudicial to the interests of good government'. The unwelcome turn of events reinforced Mazarin's conviction that the alternative to absolute monarchy was, in effect, republicanism: it was to be a recurring theme during the *Fronde*. As for Anne, in Madame de Motteville's words, 'she always wanted to ride roughshod over that court' [*Parlement*] because 'she never understood its organisation and pedantic spirit'. The initiative had passed to the extremists and the government was effectively paralysed. In the provinces people were refusing to pay their taxes. There was a rash of separate conflicts in the provinces, as local sores were inflamed by news from Paris and rivals for power no longer restrained by effective royal government. The efforts of Condé's cousin, Alais, governor of Provence, to build up a *clientèle* and to reduce the power of the *parlement* of Aix caused one sporadic local war: this was just one of several subplots in the main play. In Guienne governor Épernon was bent on settling old scores with those who had opposed his father. He had been blamed by Condé and punished by Richelieu for the defeat at Fuentarrabia. Now, wrote Guienne's *intendant*, 'He lived only for vengeance'. Here was a case where Mazarin, having no option but to exercise some control through a local grandee, seemed to have chosen badly. Yet later, Épernon would serve him well as governor of Burgundy.

Nothing is simple about the *Fronde*. If it were more than 'that sad farce' as La Rochefoucauld would call it in the bitterness of failure, it has since defied all attempts to see in it a coherent pattern or (except in the ministerial camp) a consistent ideology.

So much depended on individual character and on local circumstances. In Marseilles, Valbelle, a prominent citizen, was loyal to Mazarin and granted the right to reorganise municipal elections so as to guarantee control. When subsequently, governor Mercoeur, and *parlement*'s *premier président*, Oppède, secured a revision of the rules in their favour, Valbelle led the rebellious faction (1658–9). Louis XIV's subsequent entry into Marseilles (significantly through a breach in the walls) and a further change of rules to exclude nobles from town government, would be an early signal of his determination to control his subjects, even those of a traditionally independent city.

It would become evident that the concern of provincial sovereign courts for local power was as unappealing to the *parlement* of Paris as it was to Mazarin. *Esprit de corps* was invariably narrow in focus. Those very features of French society that made it so hard to govern, and tempted ministers to resort to arbitrary methods, made it hard to mount a concerted resistance to the policies of the crown. Meanwhile such stirrings were sufficient reason for Mazarin to offer concessions; sufficient too, since granted under duress, to let him assure the Regent that they could be revoked. They would be carried further in the declaration of Saint-Germain (October, 1648): the recall of *intendants*, for example (except in frontier provinces), and a guarantee that no individual would be deprived of office or liberty by *lettre de cachet*. Before that, Mazarin had attempted a coup, intended to deal with the extremists, which had only played into their hands. It is another episode which shows him throwing caution to the winds, trusting over-much in Parisians' respect for royal authority.

His opportunity came in August 1648 with Condé's victory at Lens and the Mass at Notre Dame held to celebrate it. At the door, troops arrested *président* Blancmesnil: of several *parlementaires* targeted he was the only one secured. The seizure of Broussel, at home, brought an angry response. The barricades went up, as much to safeguard property as to block the way to soldiers. Within days the two were released and the bargaining was resumed which led to Saint-Germain. Meanwhile Mazarin's envoys completed their diplomatic task. The Peace of Westphalia freed French troops and their commander, the still loyal Condé, for action against the *Fronde*.

The winter siege of Paris by Condé was followed by the treaty of Rueil, in March 1649, which ended the *Fronde parlementaire*. With the rebellious instinct roused, with nobles like Conti and Beaufort engaged, ostensibly in sympathy with the *Fronde* but with their own agenda; with *co-adjuteur* Gondi revelling in a situation tailor-made for his conspiratorial talents; with opportunity beckoning to former ministers like Châteauneuf and Chavigny; with *grandes dames* like Madame de Chevreuse only too willing to adopt a political role, and with some issues unresolved and radical *parlementaires* unsatisfied, Mazarin's troubles were only beginning. He was the universal scapegoat, blamed for the war against Spain, for violence against the capital and its defenders. He was vilified in a campaign of propaganda without precedent in its range, duration and virulence.

Not all the *Mazarinades* were directed against Mazarin. Some represented ministerial responses and court views. Not all were mere personal attacks. A few offered constitutional remedies. But the overwhelming impression they leave is negative: they are strong in abuse, weak in argument. It was, writes Jouhaud, 'A *Fronde* of words, not a *Fronde* of ideas'. Most pamphlets, ranging from reasoned criticism to caricature and pornography, were intended to discredit the minister, secure his removal and justify the position of whichever faction they represented. They have an important psychological role in the story. Mazarin's actions during the *Fronde* cannot be understood without taking account of the stress and discomfiture they caused. He affected to laugh with the mockers and muck-rackers. His letters, so often seeking reassurance, his moments of breakdown, as when once he wept before a deputation of *parlementaires*, and his occasionally precipitate actions should be judged in the light of his awareness of hatred, and fear of assassination. In the popular rendering Mazarin's qualities became his vices: he was handsome – so corrupting the queen-regent; clever – so not to be trusted; polite – so hypocritical. 'His name became an insult' writes Mousnier. The coachmen urged on their horses – 'or Mazarin will get you'. The composite picture given in the *Mazarinades* might appear as follows. Born to an obscure Sicilian family, his father being variously a pirate, oyster-seller or inn-keeper, he had wormed his way into Richelieu's confidence and captured the queen's affection by gifts, tricks and potions. So he ruled France from her bed. He was usurer, scrounger, charlatan, mountebank, conjuror, adventurer. In one view he was guilty of unnatural vice; in another simply effeminate. All in all it was as much popular entertainment as political criticism. The hard reality underlining it was the writers' general assumption that the monarchy would be better off without him.

In January 1649, after he had escaped from Paris with Anne and Louis, to set in motion the siege of Paris, *Parlement* tried and sentenced Mazarin, *in absentia*, to be expelled from the kingdom. In February 1651 he did go into exile at Brühl, near Cologne, and he remained there until December. At no time during these two years could he feel secure. Consistency lay only in his determination to survive and to pursue the war against Spain. More than the constant friction with *parlements* and periodic disorders in the provinces, more than the machinations of Gondi, it was the ambition of Condé that was his greatest problem.

It becomes clear with hindsight that his survival depended less on his ability to handle Condé than on Condé's talent for self-destruction. It was not evident at first – when Condé, willing to serve his king, built for himself something like an alternative ministry, with the right to veto most government appointments, deal with the dispatches in the council that would otherwise have gone to Mazarin's personal office, and even control financial policy. That was the background to the dramatic decision (January, 1650) to arrest Condé, with his brother Conti and brother-in-law Longueville. Richelieu had never shrunk from arbitrary acts but his preferred method might have been directed towards a single individual, with a trial by special court, perhaps execution. He would certainly not have attempted to justify the arrest before *Parlement*. After the arrest Mazarin, always seeking to divide and conquer, pinned his hopes on a new alliance following his reconciliation, through the good office of Madame de Chevreuse, with the powerful house of Rohan (to which she belonged) and that of Vendôme. In the 'War of the Princesses' (February–October, 1650) the Condéans were worsted. It was certain, however, that they would rally to the captive princes' cause. They had a military hero, now a martyr; a traditional cause to defend; a treacherous set of enemies to fight – and a villain to execrate.

Between October 1650 and February 1651, Mazarin made few allies but more enemies. For a time he seemed to be untypically low-spirited. In Moote's words 'the politics of duplicity had given way to the politics of indecision'. With Anne and Louis in the country on campaign – Anne deferring her return to the capital on his advice – the city was restless. With the approach of winter her delay fed hostile rumour. Lacking court patronage tradesmen were suffering. He had to cope with Condé's clients in *Parlement* and with the continuing intrigues of Gondi – more determined than ever to replace him as *premier ministre*. In November the Church Assembly demanded Conti's release (he was *abbé-général* of the order of Cluny) and refused the *don gratuit* which would have made a useful contribution to royal finances. Only where a loyal governor was in place was there the semblance of royal government or efficient collection of taxes. Mazarin's private jottings show obsessive fears, for himself and for monarchy. Events in England were influential: the deposition, trial and execution of an anointed king followed by a republic – apparently strong and confident. He could not win Molé to his cause, nor persuade *Parlement* to give up its call for the release of the princes. His main strategy was to manipulate *Parlement* through individual overtures and key appointments. In the short term, arousing mistrust, this could work against him. When the precocious and clever Nicolas Fouquet replaced the retiring *procureur-général*, his promotion was resented and his ignorance of procedures exposed.

Essentially a man of action, tiring of a waiting game which he was evidently not winning, Mazarin was relieved to get out of the hostile city and join the army in Champagne besieging Rethel. In December 1650 it beat off Turenne's attempt to relieve the city, which then surrendered. Subsequently this can be seen as a turning point. The Spanish had been shown that they could not count on the *Fronde* to paralyse the French military effort. Turenne would soon return to his allegiance. The victory was trumpeted by Mazarin's agents. But when he returned to Paris he found that it counted against him: supposedly he was pursuing the war for his own gain, and a success would mean that it would be prolonged. When Gaston, whose support he had carefully cultivated, turned against him in December 1650, he changed tack and decided to release the princes.

It is at this lowest point in Mazarin's fortunes that we can most clearly see him and Anne working as partners. Gaston had called Mazarin 'the true cause of all the disorders of the state and divisions within the royal house'. Anne knew that his unpopularity was a temporary obstacle to the restoration of order but she wished to ensure his safety and avail herself of his advice. She was looking always to the succession of her son. When he came of age (formally, at thirteen, in September, 1651) he would be the rallying point for loyal Frenchmen. In good time he would recall his loyal minister. It may be that Mazarin also had his own agenda when he rode off in person to Le Havre to see to the princes' release (February, 1651). Did he envisage gratitude? The start of a new political alignment? He met with contempt and moved off reluctantly into exile. From Brühl, in the Electorate of Cologne, he sought to direct the administration and the war.

Mazarin's daily letters from exile to ministers and to Anne often show signs of haste and agitation in their composition and style. They show him to be frustrated, insecure, anguished at the thought that his services to the crown were not properly valued – but never resigned to the possibility that he might not return. Certain main concerns stand out. Gondi was the arch-enemy 'with no other plan than to rouse sedition'. Anne should honour her commitment to secure him the cardinal's hat – it was the necessary price for his loyalty, and in due course he could be dispensed with. Condé was being given too much. Everything possible should be done to create a party among *bons bourgeois* and *honnêtes gens*. Typical among many examples is an instruction to Lionne concerning two prominent *parlementaires*: 'if you can, by whatever means possible, win over Viole and Perrault, it would be a great coup'.

Mazarin's letters have a constructive side. Besides tactical points he was defining a strategy, based on the loyalty of his chosen agents, political and military, and their mutual interest in working together for the restoration of the authority of the crown. He kept in touch with governors sympathetic to his cause, and with soldiers, like Hocquincourt, who wanted to pursue the war. He had no sympathy with Paris lawyers or grand rebels. He approached Turenne who assured him that he 'had left only to return'. It would be Turenne's mature view that 'Mazarin's designs were just and regular' whereas Richelieu's had been 'greater and less concerted'. No less important were the tactical alliances cemented by marriage bonds. The duc de Mercoeur was threatened by *Parlement* with legal action if he married Laura Mancini, the niece of the man they had proclaimed traitor and sentenced to perpetual banishment. He did so all the same. He knew that *Parlement*'s sentence would be meaningless if the king himself recalled his minister.

12

Mazarin's Triumph

The summer of 1651 brought increasing evidence that Mazarin's enemies were falling apart, that he was right to wait on events. Everywhere, but especially where armies marched and camped, there was a mood of disillusionment with all distant, or nominally legal, authority. The old parochial France of private deals and ties was reasserting itself: the man to be trusted was the local *seigneur*, who could afford protection, or the petty official who might turn a blind eye. In August the supporters of Condé and Gondi were brawling in *Parlement*. In September, Louis, the 'young Apollo' of Evelyn's phrase, came to *Parlement* to deliver his carefully rehearsed assertion of full powers. Although Anne had to appoint a new ministry, with Châteauneuf as first minister; in *surintendant* La Vieuville, the ministry contained Mazarin's choice as a man who could find acceptable ways of raising money: he followed Mazarin's advice in giving priority to the payment of salaries and interest. Chavigny was excluded, and with him Condé's hope of influencing the ministry. Le Tellier, temporarily without office, continued to work for Mazarin, reporting regularly, and receiving detailed advice.

Now it was Condé's turn to feel isolated. He discovered the difference between generalship and political leadership. In Paris his authority was disputed. He could not come to terms with the representatives of what Gondi called, with unconscious irony, 'the legitimate *fronde*'. His real influence lay in the provinces where, through his own estates, his offices, and those of his associates, he controlled a quarter of France. Basing himself on his governorship of Guienne, he lurched into rebellion. In October 1651, Louis wrote to invite Mazarin to rejoin his council. In December, with his green-scarved mercenaries, Mazarin entered France and marched towards the royal camp at Poitiers. Turenne pledged his sword to the king. Orléans joined Condé. So the lines were drawn for the last phase of the *Fronde*.

The foundation of Mazarin's growing self-confidence was his strong relationship with the young king, his godson, companion in campaign, pupil in war and politics. Louis came to see him as the victim of the ambitious rebels who, professing loyalty, had flouted royal authority. Like the king, Mazarin had suffered indignities at the hands of the people of Paris whom he had served without stint. He was conducting France's diplomatic business and was irreplaceable in that department. He was on good terms with those generals who had Louis' best interests at heart. Not least, he had built up a *clientèle* of able men, whose loyalty had survived the test of Mazarin's exile: Le Tellier, Servien and his nephew Lionne, Fouquet, soon to be *surintendant*, and his brother, the abbé Basile; not least, making himself indispensable, Colbert. In them Louis was persuaded to see the political future, when he should be restoring good government to his realm.

Meanwhile Condé had to be defeated. In the campaign of the early months of 1652, which left a swathe of destruction across France, in Condé's occupation of Paris following the battle of the Faubourg St Antoine, fought against Turenne at the city's gates in April, then in ultimate relief when Condé departed to join the Spanish, the relationship of trust between king and cardinal was sealed. They had been comrades in arms. In the end the *Fronde* came down to a military contest. On campaign, Mazarin showed courage and stamina. Directing his generals he showed a shrewd appreciation of tactics. Appreciating him as diplomat, censuring political *faux pas*, historians have tended to underplay his role as director of the royal war effort. For Louis, and the increasing numbers of *importants* who now rallied to the crown, it commended him as nothing else could have done.

Louis XIV was profoundly affected by his experience in the

Fronde – in his attitude to his greatest subjects, to *Parlement* and to Paris, the capital which he had been forced to flee, to besiege and to abandon to Condé. Out of the *Fronde* was born Versailles. He had experienced humiliation in Paris, but also ecstatic expressions of loyalty at his coming of age in September 1651, and (near-unanimously), in October 1652, at his formal entry to the city – as it were a repossession of his capital. Mazarin had come to see that Parisians were, at heart, devoted to the young sovereign. Louis had also played a part in the successes of the royal armies: soldiers appreciated his presence. Mazarin had learned the importance of presenting the king in the best possible light. His feeling for theatre comes through in carefully staged occasions: the magnificent coronation at Rheims (June, 1654), the royal wedding and subsequent parade through Paris (August, 1660). Such occasions provided a visual lesson in the great royalist themes: the king's absolute power, his special role as God's lieutenant. More important for the future was the systematic tuition of the young king in the science of government – in particular, diplomacy – where Mazarin's knowledge was unrivalled. It can indeed be said that the competent, masterful king who assumed personal rule in 1661 was Mazarin's masterpiece.

In military terms the *Fronde* could not be declared finished until August 1653, when white Mazarinist flags replaced the red in Bordeaux, marking its surrender and the end of the *Ormée*, a revolutionary movement exceptional in its civic radicalism, and as unwelcome to Condé as it was to the crown. By then Condé was with the Spanish in Flanders, still posing a military threat – but also an argument for loyalty to the crown. The strength of the reaction against the *Fronde*, the war-weariness, the longing for peace, stability and normal trading conditions, the disgrace of the principal rebels and positive enthusiasm for the king, have led historians to see the fall of Bordeaux as a mere postscript to the *Fronde*; also the *lit de justice* that followed the royal entry in October 1652, as a cleaner break and tidier end than was seen by those best able to judge at the time. Ministers knew that much of the *frondeur* spirit lived on.

'Henceforth members are prohibited from taking any cognisance of the general affairs of the state and the direction of finances.' The words of the king at that *lit de justice* at suggest a crushing defeat for *Parlement*. The reality was different.

71

Notably missing was any repudiation of the specific reforms of four years ago. The crown would claw back powers, especially through the restoration of *intendants*. Mazarin's administration would continue to be as absolutist in spirit as Richelieu's. The letters of Séguier, Le Tellier, perhaps especially Colbert, constantly on the alert for signs of trouble, leave no doubt about that. But Séguier was now more sensitive to the claims of the sovereign courts; the trend towards conciliar justice was halted. Fouquet, by nature a pragmatist, was content to work within the system that rewarded him so handsomely. Obstacles were to be got round, not taken by storm. The institutional legacy of the *Fronde* was the preservation of the entrenched corporate society, with its overlapping jurisdictions and franchises.

The moderation espoused by Molé throughout and, latterly, by most senior *parlementaires*, helped create an atmosphere in which it was possible for both sides, ministers and magistrates, to envisage compromise. There was no realistic alternative. The letter of the law, as pronounced in edicts, says little about the general state of mind. Constitutional history has to take account of the dynamic forces in a given situation. That of the first years after the *Fronde* was volatile. *Parlement* was periodically obstructive. The exiled Retz, supported by the Pope, maintained his contacts with sympathetic Parisian clergy. Jansenism had political overtones. 'He has always been seditious' observed Mazarin, seeing the connection with Jansenism for which the firebrand Roch was expelled from the Sorbonne (1656). In the provinces, particularly in the west, meetings of noblemen were watched with concern. Many of them had been disappointed by the crown's failure to honour its pledge of 1650 to summon a States-General. Judging from the *cahiers* prepared for that assembly, there would have been wide-ranging criticism of the whole system of government associated with the cardinals.

The mood of ministers was necessarily cautious. Vengeful instincts were kept in check – to Mazarin's credit. He had helped smooth the way for the royal entry by a voluntary second exile, in August 1652. He had not hurried to return. When he did, in February 1653, he found acceptance beyond court and *clientèle*. He was given credit by many Parisians for his role in the royal restoration. Focusing again on the central aim, the defeat of Spain, he showed how much he had learned from his experiences during the *Fronde*. Certain leading rebels, Broussel and Viole for example, were exiled. Most were soon forgiven. In Restoration England (post-1660), so limited a purge would look decidedly moderate. Mazarin worked quietly to extend his *clientèle*. He allowed increasing scope to ministers, notably Le Tellier and Fouquet, now *surintendant*. When the smack of firm government was required, as after *Parlement* had insisted on discussing edicts already registered, he could rely on Louis to deliver it: on 13 April, 1655, the king descended on *Parlement*, still in his morning hunting clothes, and warned the magistrates to stay within bounds: 'I have come here expressly to forbid you to carry on. . .'.

One episode illustrates how vulnerable Mazarin could still be, how difficult it was (as Charles II would soon find) to maintain a post-war balance of reward when the means of gratification were insufficient to meet demand. Harcourt, a successful soldier, hitherto loyal, took himself off to Breisach and there negotiated with the Emperor for an independent principality. After a year of negotiation, during which Mazarin bought the services of the Philippsburg garrison and paid off the Breisach mercenaries, Harcourt came to terms. He received back all his offices and the governorships of Upper and Lower Alsace, since the king 'wished to show goodwill in restoring affairs to M. de Harcourt in the condition that they were in before'. How much of the *Fronde*, of the constraints within which Mazarin had to operate, of the bargaining basis of 'absolute' government – indeed of French history – is contained in that episode!

13

The Making of Peace

Peace had been talked about since Mazarin first came to France.
Both Pope Urban and Richelieu had envisaged him as playing a
leading part in the process – though from different standpoints.
Since 1641, when Swedish and French envoys had met at
Hamburg, committed themselves not to make a separate peace,
and discussed preliminaries, there had ensued delays and pre-
varications. It was not until December 1644 that the Congress
of Münster opened with pompous ceremony and procedural
gambits designed to convey the intention and capacity of all
concerned to hold out for the best possible terms.The final
treaties of Münster and Osnabrück that comprised the Peace of
Westphalia were not signed till October 1648. Bluff and bargaining round the table reflected the fluctuating fortunes of war.
After the Emperor's defeat at the second battle of Breitenfeld
(November, 1642), and Spain's at Rocroi (June, 1643), Maximilian of Bavaria had a strong hand. It became clear that the
Habsburg alliance was damaging both partners: so Ferdinand
sanctioned negotiations. The near destruction of Spain's army
at Flanders put the issue of Dutch independence beyond doubt;
it only remained to decide exactly where – between the United
Provinces and the Spanish Netherlands – the frontier should be
drawn. It did not, however, immediately signal the end of
hostilities in Flanders, let alone the end of the German War.

The war of 1644 between Sweden and Denmark brought

Ferdinand short-lived relief and hope. The victorious Swedes resumed their aggressive course in 1645. Queen Christina urged her envoy to press Swedish claims without delaying the peace. The Swedish alliance typifies the kind of problem Mazarin faced, like Richelieu before him. If Sweden made a separate peace the Emperor would be fighting on one front instead of two. An effective French war effort depended on cooperation with the Swedes. However, this jeopardised good relations with Catholic Bavaria, which Mazarin sought to detach from Austria. It also offended the *dévôts*, whom Mazarin needed to impress, as a man striving for a Christian peace.

Other difficulties were caused by the possibility that Spain and the United Provinces would make a separate peace. Mazarin contributed to them. Always susceptible to the lure of the grand design, he proposed that Philip IV should exchange the Spanish Netherlands for French-occupied Catalonia. 'The satisfaction with which he outlined his plan leads one to think that he was intoxicated by its beauty' wrote Lionne. Unfortunately it raised questions about a previous undertaking, that the French and Dutch would engage in the conquest of Flanders. By making overtures to the *stadholder* Frederick Henry about the transfer of Antwerp to the Dutch, he made matters worse. He did not allow for the tension between the republican-inclined States-General and the *stadholder*, nor the jealous concern of Amsterdam traders about a revival of Antwerp, nor the suspicion of Dutch Protestants aroused by the sympathy shown in French *dévôt* circles to Dutch Catholics. 'Ally, not neighbour' was the general view of Dutchmen towards France. Predictably the Spanish revealed Mazarin's plan to the Dutch. That at once created a climate favourable to the separate negotiation that Mazarin feared, and which led to the treaty of Münster in January 1648.

In a letter to Servien, Mazarin reveals how his mind was working:

'The acquisition of the Spanish Netherlands would give the city of Paris an impregnable rampart and it could then truly be called the heart of France. . . . So much money and blood would be well spent if . . . provinces were annexed which, in the past, have provided the means to rulers . . . to trouble France to the extent which we all know.'

It might have been Turenne writing, or, later, Vauban. The tone was hawkish – and Mazarin, like Turenne, saw advantages to outweigh cost and danger in pursuing the war against Spain after Westphalia. But the emphasis was essentially defensive, reflecting the experience of the 'year of Corbie'. One day Vauban would be commissioned to create a fortress ring round France. The opportunity would come with the series of acquisitions, starting in 1648. The targets chosen for negotiation, and the gains secured, suggest a realistic military policy, like Richelieu's, giving priority to existing strongpoints and defensible sites.

The German issues had been complicated from the start of the war. Most of the German states had, by now, made their peace with the Emperor. Several, like Brandenburg and the Palatinate, had outstanding claims. The expectations of the warring powers, principally now Austria, Bavaria, Sweden and France, had risen with the length of time they had been at war. Negotiation was bound to be long and difficult. When, after a year, delegates sought to define the issues, they grouped them under four heads: the complaints of the Imperial Estates, the conditions of amnesty for rebels, satisfaction of foreign allies, and compensation of the dispossessed. After 1643, Mazarin followed Richelieu's careful and detailed instructions: in themselves they are a monument to Richelieu's lofty sense of what could be justified – and attained. They express his characteristic view of a stateman's duty, in the temporal world, to create order. That meant a lasting and general peace, a French peace for the good of Christendom, to be protected by the formation of two leagues, in Germany and Italy. A system of collective security was thus one of two objectives of a continuing policy; the other was the acquisition of bases and points of access. Common to both was the assumption, which has aroused in equal measure praise for far-sightedness and censure for hypocrisy (Pope Urban's view), that the interests of France were also those of Germany, therefore of Europe. The German states had suffered cruelly from a civil war which had exposed them to invasion from the outside. Now there were German princes ready to envisage France as guarantor of peace.

The framework for negotiation, and its objectives, had been set out by Richelieu. Its implementation was entirely Mazarin's responsibility. From the start he was in control. The Venetian ambassador, Nani, expressed the contemporary view when he wrote: 'the absolute direction of the kingdom, of the forces, of the arms, of the treasury all depend on the will of the Cardinal'. Certainly, in matters of diplomacy, he encountered little serious opposition in council. His were the final decisions. In Longueville, titular head of the diplomatic mission, d'Avaux, idealistic, experienced and skilful, and above all Servien, a tough and realistic negotiator, he had a well-balanced team. Their commitment, backed by unanimity in council, enabled him to defy opponents and to maintain a stiff negotiating stance. When d'Avaux and Servien quarrelled, Mazarin relied mainly on Servien, backed by Lionne, Servien's nephew. As Anne's secretary, Lionne was well placed to ensure easy communication and prompt decision.

Mazarin was assured, for a few years, of sufficient revenue to support military operations. Indeed the level of expenditure between 1643 and 1645 was the highest to date. Richelieu might have been more sensitive than Mazarin to the grievances of those injured by Particelli's ingenious financial measures. There is, however, as little value in speculating whether Richelieu would have found means to hasten the peace, as in pondering whether he would have avoided the *Fronde*. What is certain is that Mazarin justified Richelieu's confidence, negotiated with great skill, gave clear instructions to his emissaries, kept his nerve when things went wrong, and capitalised, as well as could be expected, on the occasional successes of his generals.

It can be argued that diplomats could no longer control the war, that it was the war that controlled them. That is not the impression given by Mazarin's correspondence, an impressive record of the pursuit of a longed-for peace, with gains sufficient to justify the cost of war. 'He was the man for the hour . . . when diplomacy and war went hand in hand' (Livet). To some extent the Peace of Westphalia was bound to be a compromise. Mazarin had to balance potentially conflicting aims: the peace for Christian Europe which had been his Papal brief and a strategic frontier for the security of France. Throughout the protracted negotiations he had to take into account opinion at home. One motive for the Cinq Mars and *Importants* conspiracies had been the belief that the fall, respectively, of Richelieu and Mazarin, would mean the end of the war. When, to impress the Habsburgs, Mazarin gave the impression that he could negotiate for ever, he laid himself open to the domestic charge that he was pursuing the war for private gain. When critics, like Talon in January 1648, stressed the urgent need for peace, they weakened his bargaining position. Several French demands, like the Emperor's counter-claims, were put forward as negotiating positions: not all were tenable. In the end it was not just what was gained at Westphalia that was significant, but what the gains would lead to, particularly in terms of French influence in Germany. Mazarin realised that Westphalia was not the end, but the start of a continuing process of extending French influence in Germany.

A start was made when he broke the northern deadlock, satisfied one ally and found another, by the division of Pomerania. To compensate him for losing to Sweden the more valuable western part, Elector Frederick William of Brandenburg was allotted Halberstadt, Minden and the reversion to Magdeburg. In March 1647 Maximilian of Bavaria signed the treaty of Ulm, trusting in Mazarin's assurance of support for his claim to the Upper Palatinate. Before the end of the year which saw mutinies cripple the French armies, he was back in Leopold's camp. Against the background of *parlementaire* protest, Mazarin's campaign plans for 1648 could have seemed foolhardy. In May, however, Turenne linked with Wrangel to defeat the imperialists at Zusmarshausen, Maximilian reverted to the Treaty of Ulm and that brought further pressure on the Emperor. The archduke Leopold's defeat at Lens led Mazarin to deliver the coup against opposition leaders which provoked the *Fronde* and persuaded him to instruct his envoys to settle. By October the Swedes were besieging Prague. The Emperor too was ready to come to terms.

The new balance of power in the north, following Mazarin's deliberate promotion of Brandenburg, would suit France well. At the treaty of Oliva, in 1660, concluding the Northern War which began with Charles X's invasion of Poland, Mazarin's envoys would be welcomed arbiters. Sweden's position in Germany would now be a defensive one. In the south a stronger Maximilian, finally indebted for the Upper Palatinate more to France than to the Emperor, could be expected to be an ally. Geography, strategy and material interests combined to persuade the rulers of the truncated Palatinate, restored Trier and friendly Cologne and Mainz that France would be their natural patron. There had been little difficulty about the confirmation of sovereignty over Metz, Toul and Verdun, held since 1559. It was Alsace that had provided the most severe test. There, patient diplomacy achieved the best outcome, short of complete annexation.

After its flank had been secured by the capture of Breisach in 1638, Alsace had been the base for offensive operations. Richelieu had pledged that France would respect particular liberties and would not consider permanent annexation. However it soon became unthinkable that France would throw away her advantage. In December 1647 Mazarin wrote to Turenne: 'I trust that you consider Alsace a country which belongs to the king no less than does Champagne'. Bidding high, he claimed, first, the whole territory, with Philippsburg, Breisach and some smaller towns besides. In bargaining the last were dropped, but he stood firm for Philippsburg and Breisach, and succeeded. Alsace was diverse in language, laws, forms and degrees of sovereignty, with allegiance to the Emperor generally indirect or nominal: there were seven distinct political entities. In its gaps and ambiguities, the disposal of Alsace reflected the variety which Servien, encouraged by Mazarin, strove to exploit. France was accorded the 'prefecture' over ten Alsatian towns, but without sovereign control. The Sundgau, in Southern Alsace, was granted without reservation. Mazarin had to accept second best, with the imprecise formulas and limited gains which emerged from Servien's wrangling. The latter's view was complacent: 'I believe that we shall have to be content that everyone should keep their claims and interpret the treaty as they see fit'. For the ultimate disposal of the rest of Alsace, two blank cheques were left: the future would depend on the relative state of Austria and France. As the Imperialist Isaac Volmar said, 'the stronger will win'. 'Stronger' for a time meant the Habsburgs, whose raids between 1649 and 1657 showed aggressive intent. Fulfilment of Volmar's prophecy would come in 1681, when Louis XIV's troops marched into Strasburg and completed the process by which he gained sovereignty over Alsace.

Mazarin's Alsatian manoeuvres have to be seen in the context of his view of the French interest in Germany: such a degree of security as was compatible with good relations with neighbouring princes. During the *Fronde*, France benefited – from the goodwill earned in the Rhineland – as did Mazarin personally during his months of exile. After the *Fronde* he exploited the growing value of French patronage. He was emboldened to think, even, that some electors might abandon their traditional loyalty to the Habsburgs. In 1657, after Ferdinand's death, Mazarin sent a strong French embassy to promote the claims of Louis XIV. He had faith in gold 'distributed liberally and carefully' and wished he could find more: for then one 'could do such great things as it would be hard to hope for in several centuries'. He was not surprised at the outcome: to make a non-German Emperor 'would be much like aspiring to defeat a great fleet with two or three brigantines'.

The electors voted unanimously for the Habsburg Leopold. They did not vote for a stronger Emperor. Under French persuasion they imposed further restrictions on his authority. Backed by Mazarin, von Schönborn, archbishop-elector of Mainz and Imperial Chancellor, created the confederation of princes to safeguard the liberties of Germany which would be called the League of the Rhine. Instituted in 1658 it was the positive answer to the question arising out of the history of the previous 40 years: how to secure the rights of those small states when the Emperor himself breached the constitution and foreign princes seized German lands? By ensuring the membership of France, along with that of Sweden, Mazarin served both Germany and France. Besides France and Sweden the League first included the Electors of Mainz and Cologne, three Brunswick dukes and the Landgrave of Hesse-Cassel. With its permanent directory at Frankfort and a treasury well supplied with French money, in Hauser's words, it 'extended the true frontier of France, that of political influence, beyond the territorial frontier to the Rhine'. So Mazarin taught his royal pupil a lesson in statecraft – imperfectly learned and followed.

Future patterns can be seen emerging from Westphalia. Mazarin's career coincided with the decline in the political influence of the Papacy which he had earlier served. The Pope could do no more now than denounce the treaty as 'null and void'. Brandenburg had the potential to balance the intrusive presence of Sweden. Holland would exercise its strength in world markets. Spain would continue to decline and there would be a reorientation in Austria's policy, as emperors faced the Ottoman challenge and concentrated more on the hereditary lands: correspondingly France had the chance to dominate.

England's temporary isolation was due, however, to temporary circumstances. Since 1642 and the outbreak of civil war there had been no coherent English foreign policy. After his defeat at the battle of Worcester (1651), Charles II's political stock declined into insignificance. Legitimacy weighed more with Anne than with Mazarin. For him the essential fact, measured by the authority of his government and the size of his army, was the power of Cromwell – after 1653 Lord Protector – and, some thought, would-be-king. England's mercantile interests led her to war with Holland (1652–4). It brought material gains. The English held that they were 'perfectly lords and masters of the narrow seas'. England's natural enemy, however, on traditional Protestant grounds, was Spain.

In 1656 Spain made a treaty with Charles II and offered to finance a small royalist force. This invited Cromwell's retaliation. Logic pointed then to alliance with France – and Mazarin needed an ally. Spain had not capitalised fully on the *Fronde*. However, her soldiers had some successes, notably the capture of Barcelona, which effectively ended the Catalan revolt. In the same year, 1652, they recaptured Graveslines and Dunkirk. Spain had already choked off the chance of peace with France in 1648. As the *Fronde* developed don Haro's negotiating stance stiffened. The defection of Condé brought further encouragement. He under-estimated Mazarin's resolution. In 1653 Mazarin took personal charge of the war effort. His letters from Sedan show him supervising strategy and supplies. Turenne's successful sieges of Flemish towns were not, however, enough to bring Spain to seek peace. In 1656 Condé showed disconcerting strength and gained new adherents. After 'the misfortune of Valenciennes' (Condé had relieved its siege in July, 1656), Mazarin decided to grasp the nettle.

A republican and radical Protestant, Cromwell was anathema to Catholics and royalists. An English alliance would be a propaganda gift to Condé, Retz and their supporters. Mazarin had been vehement in his denunciation of the English regicides but he had offered few favours to the widowed Henrietta Maria, living uncomfortably in Paris. Carefully tutored by Mazarin, Louis was persuaded that his country's interest required the alliance. The English 'redcoats' could secure victory – and peace. After months of negotiation a treaty was signed in Paris in March 1657. Joint action was planned in Flanders:

Graveslines was promised to France, Dunkirk and Mardyke to England. The ensuing campaign brought swift justification. The combined French and English force defeated Condé's army at the battle of the Dunes (June, 1658). Turenne went on to seize Flemish towns. Her treasure fleet seized by Blake, her army defeated by the Portuguese at Elvas, Spain contemplated peace at last. Philip IV's priority was now to hold on to Portugal. That gave Mazarin a crucial bargaining weapon. Also useful to him was the Spanish sense of honour and obligation to an ally. To him Condé was a dangerous traitor, to the Spanish an ally: for his honourable reinstatement, and for the restoration of duke Charles to Lorraine, they would make concessions. Knowing that a further campaign would yield still more Flemish towns, Mazarin preferred not to use France's clear military advantage to strengthen his diplomatic hand. He undertook not to aid the rebels in Portugal and the talks were preceded by a ceasefire.

After four months of fierce bargaining the 124 articles which comprise the Peace of the Pyrenees (1659) delivered to France Artois, the Pyrenean provinces of Cerdagne and Roussillon, the county of Bar and the right of military passage through Lorraine (in return for the duke's restoration), and terms for the marriage of Louis XIV to the Infanta of Spain, Maria Teresa. For this vital contract Mazarin gave up both his earlier hope of a marriage alliance with a Savoyard princess and the tempting possibility, for the fame of the family, of the match that Louis himself so keenly desired with his niece Marie Mancini. Mazarin had to use strong words to persuade the king to let her go: 'I urge you for your glory, your honour, for the well-being of the realm'; again, 'your passions should yield to that you should have, to be a king, so wise and capable of governing your realm that you are great and already very glorious'. Grammar and style can be faulted, as so often with Mazarin, who wrote, as he thought, in a rush. The message is clear. The compensating glory would be great, the prospect boundless.

As his contribution to the marriage settlement, Louis renounced all claims to the Spanish throne, on condition that the Infanta's dowry was paid: it was fixed at 500,000 gold *écus* to be paid in three instalments. The sum would be beyond the resources of Spain's treasury. Non-payment would become the pretext for 'The War of the Queen's Rights', launched in 1667. Then the easy progress of French troops and further gains by treaty would confirm the general view of the Treaty of the Pyrenees: there had occurred a decisive alteration in the balance of power. It was the greatest achievement of the cardinals.

14

Reputations

When Richelieu died, in December 1642, his only request to the king was that the kingdom should 'continue to honour my nephews and kinsmen with its protection and good will'. After valuable bequests to the crown, notably the Palais Cardinal, which now became the Palais Royal, he set up entails, based on his two duchies, to preserve his estate for his designated heir, his great-nephew, Armand-Jean de Pont-Courlay. Quarrels within the family, and the crown's failure to pay its debts to the estate, meant that the four million *livres* which the cardinal had kept in cash for emergencies proved insufficient for legacies and for his designated projects, notably the completion of the chapel and college of the Sorbonne. Ambition to establish his family among the highest in the land, service to the crown, and a respect for religion and scholarship: in death, as in life, the main themes emerge, inviting a range of judgements almost as wide today as it was in his lifetime.

News of his death was greeted with bonfires in the provinces, where his ministry was associated with higher taxes, repression where there had been revolt, and the dreaded billetting of troops: all the effect of war, generally seen as his war. For the next 200 years, the prevailing view continued to be hostile. In his memoirs Retz, predictably, held that he 'blasted rather than governed'. Le Vassor, writing in 1712, summarised the *dévôt* case, originating in Richelieu's break with Marillac, which had been sealed later by the authority of Fénelon and become a kind of orthodoxy among those who deplored the growth in the power of the state and its tendency to aggressive war: that he sacrificed the liberty of his fatherland and the peace of all Europe to his ambition. For the absolutist generation of Colbert, who matched Richelieu's vision and developed his projects, he had been 'the great cardinal'. That only strengthened the *dévôt* case when Colbertism, leading to more intense competition between states and therefore to war, became discredited during Louis XIV's later years. Growing out of the *fin de siècle* period of defeats and disillusion the Enlightenment inherited that view and added its own flavours of cultural relativism and religious scepticism. Montesquieu saw *parlementaire* privilege and the particularism of the *pays d'etats* as guarantors of liberty against an oppressive state. To the author of *L'Esprit des Lois*, Richelieu, unsurprisingly, was 'un méchant citoyen'. To Voltaire he was a tyrant who made war because he wanted to make himself necessary. Nor did he fare better with the romantic generation. From Alfred de Vigny to Dumas, it was a monster of cruelty and depravity that was presented to readers avid for sensation. The nineteenth-century historian Michelet called him the 'dictator of despair'. The word 'dictator' would have a new resonance in twentieth-century Europe, colouring even the sober judgement of so fine a historian as David Ogg, who wrote that 'men of his type will always triumph so long as cold, calculating intellect can overcome passion and sentiment'.

It should be noticed that each judgement reflects the attitude of the time and the position of the author; also that no one attempted to minimise Richelieu's importance. If he was a bad man he was also a great man. When Richelieu found admirers there was the same tendency to exaggerate, as historians found in his policies what fitted their political view. For Buonapartists and neo-absolutists, he was to be revered for his self-sacrificing, single-minded service to the state. Had he not said on his deathbed that he had 'no enemies but those of the state'? Gradually another kind of orthodoxy became established – given authority by the massive labours of Hanotaux. 'He completed French unity through the final establishment of the king's absolute authority and the ruin of the House of Spain'. A reinforcement to what might be termed the twentieth-century patriotic view came with the wars against Germany between

85

1870 and 1945, in relation for example to the fate of Alsace and Lorraine. It was the authoritarian aspect of his policies, however, that made him an icon of the right, responsible for a concentration of authority which might be compared with that achieved by Mussolini – in the view of Bailly (1934). Even after the more balanced post-war assessment of Tapié and the feeding in of research about seventeenth-century France, particularly its provinces, the British or American reader may be tempted to feel that the real Richelieu needed to be rescued from his countrymen and their ideological standpoint.

To that 'real' picture detail is being added all the time. The work of Bonney, in the field of government, notably the *intendants*; Kettering, dealing with social and political mores and structures (notably *clientèles*); Parker, Beik and Mettam on absolutism and, most relevantly to this study, Bergin, on Richelieu's ascent to power – to give only a few examples out of many – has made it possible to judge his career in relation to the society which moulded his attitudes. In this approach, well-grounded in evidence though it has been, there is an inherent danger. In reaction to the twin ideas – of Richelieu as 'founder', or even chief promoter, of absolutism – and of absolutism as a system more complete and powerful than it could possibly have been, there has been a tendency to devalue the heroic, compelling nature of the man, and the scale of his achievement. The way in which Richelieu developed his fortune and power base is revealing, but it is the use he made of it that is ultimately most important. That is no less impressive for being set in the context of troubled times and imperfect systems of government; his quality is not diminished by revelation of his moments of weakness. The student of Richelieu may not warm to him. He must surely find much to admire in his faith, courage and imagination.

Mazarin died in March 1661. The circumstances were more favourable to his immediate reputation than those of 1642. There was peace, and a young king ready to assume power – an undisputed power. He died with a humble and contrite spirit, after a rigorous course of preparation with a priest who obeyed his wish to be treated like any other penitent, 'knowing that there is but one gospel for the great and lowly alike'. He had shown stoical courage in working to the end. He died a very rich man, with possessions that have been valued at 39 million *livres* (Richelieu's fortune was 22 million). He wished to bequeath the bulk of his fortune to the king; only when that was refused did he make provision for his family. Of that fortune no less than a third was in the form of realisable assets, coin, bullion and precious stones, stored in Paris and other carefully selected strongholds. Like Richelieu he had acquired large church revenues, with the income of 24 abbeys. He had three duchies. He had bought paintings, tapestries and furniture shrewdly in a depressed market. Undoubtedly he had benefited from the absence of proper auditing and the direct availability of funds to secure money for himself. Gratified that Fouquet was restoring credit (though only about 30 per cent of the levies extracted was available, as revenue, to the crown), he appears to have been sunnily indifferent to the disciplines of financial management, happy to take advantage of its laxity. Serving him as his man of business, screwing out of his property an increasing income from his lands and rights, Colbert had learned enough about the abuses of the financial system to enable him, as Louis XIV's *contrôleur-général*, to instigate a severe regime of reform.

There we have some of the materials for later judgements of Mazarin: the adventurer, ensuring against downfall with a huge private cache; the insatiable collector, greedy miser; the casually unscrupulous minister, master of the private deal, the sugared pill; also, however, the devoted royal servant, the loyal *patron*, the patient negotiator, and the man of peace who could boast that he had delivered it – and to France's advantage.

Such verdicts are not necessarily contradictory. Mazarin could be, in some degree all of those things. It is what the Carmelite monk Léon depicted in an obituary sermon, describing 'the lights and shade' in his career and 'the mysterious enigma' of the whole:

> 'He was French and Italian, soldier and doctor of law, layman and cardinal, foreigner and royal servant, exile and pleni-potentiary, subject and friend of the king; a most notable victim, a phoenix; a Phoebus after the clouds have rolled away; the arbiter of great peoples and nations.'

The enigmatic Mazarin has continued to tease historians. Their verdicts will depend on the position from which they start – Goubert's, for example, from the *Annales* school of social history, Dethan's from special interest in the Italian background and influences, Laurain-Portemer's from her deep knowledge of the cultural scene and his response to it. Stress on the materialist side, or on his concern for the promotion of his family, may convey an impression of a man far Richelieu's inferior, near to the caricatures of the *Mazarinades*. As with Richelieu, Mazarin's reputation suffered from the *dévôt* opposition to a foreign policy which led to war with Spain, given further stress by the misfortunes of war in the last decades of Louis XIV's reign – that ageing Louis, who had been schooled by Mazarin in the 'Machiavellianism' which was the main charge of Fénelon's influential *Dialogue des Morts*. His overall achievement received, however, a convincing reappraisal in Chéruel's immense history of the Minority (four volumes, 1879), reinforced by his nine-volume edition of his letters. The view (Dethan's notably) of Mazarin as the good European, seeker of a Christian peace – which is not, we have seen, inconsistent with a view of him as a good Frenchman – has particular appeal to the Europe-minded Frenchmen of today.

The treaties of Westphalia and the Pyrenees are an impressive memorial. Judgement by 'results', without reference to context or cost, may, at first, seem to elevate Mazarin beyond his deserts. He is still, in some ways, an elusive figure, since the records are patchy: voluminous for the conduct of diplomacy and war, revealing of certain private thoughts in his *carnets*, but frustratingly thin for his involvement in the domestic scene, in particular for decisions in council. Yet sober judgement may allow that he belonged to the small group of statesmen who have succeeded in their main objectives and affected the course of history. He saw monarchy emerge from its ordeals stronger in powers and esteem. He was responsible, through arduous negotiations, for treaties which extended the boundaries of France, provided a degree of security for the future, together with the distinct possibility of a great inheritance to come. It was no accident that after his mentor's death the young Louis was able to assume personal rule, the best schooled and, in his grasp of the business of government, most competent of sovereigns. Nor that through carefully choreographed ceremonies, the people were conditioned to accept an exalted style of kingship, divinely ordained and lifted above ordinary mortals. Nor that he started his rule with a talented group of ministers who had learned their trade in service with the cardinal, combining the self-interested cohesion of the *clientèle* with dedication to the interests of the state.

Glossary

Aides	A variety of indirect taxes, mostly on drink, levied by the state
Arrêts	Royal orders not requiring registration to give them immediate force of law
Avocat-général	One of crown's representatives in *Parlement*
Bourgeoisie	Non-noble members of the upper echelons of – usually urban – society, sufficiently well-off not to do manual work and possessed of privileges – as opposed to the mere *habitant*
Cahiers	Submissions by electors to be considered by a States-General
Carnets	Mazarin's notebooks containing his jottings, often when travelling, or in haste: a valuable guide to his private thoughts and fears
Chambre de Justice	Special financial court set up to confiscate financiers' gains and to teach political lessons
Clientèle	In political usage a close-knit group of dependants, bound to the patron by mutual interest in advancement
Co-adjuteur	Ecclesiastical title, denoting an assistant to a bishop
Code Michau	Named after its author, Michel de Marillac: a wide-ranging unwieldy compilation defining areas of law in which government was involved and laying down principles and rules

Commissaire	An official provided with a commission to undertake specified duties in a *généralité*
Conseil d'état	The original royal council out of which have evolved, with the growth of government, several bodies with specialised functions and, by Louis XIV's reign, the executive council, *le conseil d'en haut*
Conseil de conscience	Council for religious affairs – first met regularly during regency of Anne
Corvée	Statutory labour required by custom
Créature	In political usage a person in dependent but well-established relationship to the *patron*
Croquant	A clod-hopper; name for peasant-rebels
Curés	Parish priest
Dauphin	Title of the heir-presumptive to the throne
Dérogeance	Loss of status by nobles participating in certain occupations – notably (with a few exceptions) manufactures and trades
Dévôt	Member of zealous Catholic party opposed to toleration for Huguenots, tending towards a pro-Spanish foreign policy
Duc et pair	Nobleman of the highest rank, also enjoying the privileges of a peer (as possessor of a fief erected into a *duché-pairie*) as distinct from mere *duc*
Élection	Fiscal area presided over by an *élu*, responsible for apportioning the *taille* on the basis of personal income
Élu(s)	Tax officials presiding over a fiscal area in an election, responsible for apportioning the *taille* on the basis of personal income
Enquêtes	One of the three main chambers of *Parlement*
États-généraux/ Estates-general	A meeting of deputies of the three orders, Church, Nobility and *Tiers état*. Met in 1614–15, not again till 1789
Fermier	Leasehold, responsible, for a fee or proportion of proceeds, for collecting dues, seigneurial or royal
Fronde	The name given (after *fronde*, a sling) to the series of rebellions of 1648–53. Also *frondeur*, a participant in the *Fronde*

Gabelles	Salt taxes levied on a basis which varied according to regions, exemptions and privileges
Généralité	One of major administrative regions (23 in 1643) into which the country was divided; becoming the seat of the *intendances*;
Les Grands	Collectively, an informal name for the highest nobles
Intendant	Royal commissary (see *maître des requêtes*), empowered to oversee financial, administrative affairs in the provinces; the *intendant de l'armée* had a more specialised function but matters of discipline and supply had implications for the civilians in his field of operations
Lèse-majesté	High treason
Lettre de cachet	A letter emanating from the sovereign, signed by a *secrétaire d'étât*, containing an order relative to an individual (commonly for imprisonment), or a particular case
Lit de justice	Ceremony in which the king, attending personally, could enforce registration of edicts in *Parlement* or other sovereign courts
Livre	Money of account, comprising twenty *sous*, a *sou*, 12 *déniers* (as L.S.D.)
Maître des Requêtes	A royal judge attached to the *conseil du roi*; often first step to higher office; *intendants* usually drawn from *maîtres*
Mazarinades	Pamphlets written during the *Fronde*, mainly against Mazarin
Menu peuple	The common people, often used in a derogatory sense
Noblesse d'épée	Nobility of the sword: the military, not necessarily ancient nobility, privileged, supposedly, by virtue of feudal service
Noblesse de robe	Nobility derived from office in the higher ranks of the judiciary and administration
Office	A permanent government post (as distinct from a temporary commission (see *Intendants*): generally for sale (see *paulette*), sometimes conferring nobility. *Officier*, holder of office
Parlement	Sovereign, final court of appeal, having three

courts – *Grand Chambre, Enquêtes* and *Requêtes*, with wide powers of police (latter word conveying both justice and administration). The *parlement* of Paris (in text simply *Parlement*) had jurisdiction over more than a third of the realm, with responsibility for registering royal edicts. Besides that of Paris there were nine provincial *parlements* in 1643: Toulouse, Bordeaux, Grenoble, Dijon, Rouen, Aix, Rennes, Pau, and (1633) Metz

Paulette or *droit annuel*   A form of premium enabling an *officier* to transmit his office in return for one-sixtieth of its estimated value. Its renewal gave scope for bargaining between crown and *officiers*

Place de sûreté   A town allowed, by the terms of the Edict of Nantes, to have a Huguenot garrison

Politique   Term used, notably in the Religious Wars, denoting one who might put French political concerns before those of religious allegiance; also, more broadly, *bons français* (opp. *dévôts*)

Premier président   Presides over *Grand Chambre* of *Parlement*; only post in *Parlement* (not an office but a *charge* and revocable) nominated by the king.

Procureur-général   One of the *gens du roi*, royal representatives in *Parlement*

Receveurs   Officials responsible locally for collection of taxes

Rentes   A government bond issued on the security of municipal revenues; a *rentier* as the recipient of such revenue

Secrétaire d'état   From original secretarial role holders of this venal office have become heads of ministerial departments, with responsibility for designated *généralités*. Only those summoned to sit regularly in the *conseil d'en haut* (q.v.) were designated *ministres*

Sol pour livre   A 5 per cent sales tax introduced in 1640

Subsistances   A tax paid by townspeople to exempt them from billetting troops

Surintendant des finances   Head of the financial administration

Taille	The main direct tax: levied both on income – the *taille personelle*, applicable to the *pays d'élection* (c.v.) – or on property – *taille réelle* in the *pays d'états* (c.v.)
Testament Politique	In part written or dictated by Richelieu and following, overall, his general plan: a valuable source for his ideas and policies
Toisé	A tax (1643: after resistance abortive) on houses in the suburbs of Paris
Traitants	Financiers who had made a contract, or *traité* with the crown: usually to levy taxes or sell offices
Trésoriers de France	Financial officials who headed the *bureaux des finances* in each *généralité*

Further Reading

Revealing documents can be studied in two collections:

Richard Bonney (ed.), *Society and Government under Richelieu and Mazarin* (Macmillan, 1988)

J.H. Shennan, *Government and Society in France, 1461–1661* (Allen and Unwin, 1972)

To provide the setting and to give further detail:

Robin Briggs, *Early Modern France, 1560–1715* (Oxford, 1977)

Peter Campbell, *The Ancien Régime in France* (Blackwell, 1988)

James B. Collins, *The State in Early Modern France* (Cambridge, 1995)

P. Goubert, *The Ancien Régime* (1969, trans. Weidenfeld, 1973)

R. Mandrou, *Introduction to Modern France* (Arnold, 1975)

Orest Ranum, *The Fronde – a French Revolution* (Norton, 1993)

V.L. Tapié, *France in the Reign of Louis XIII and Richelieu* (1952, trans Cambridge, 1984)

G.R.R. Treasure, *Seventeenth Century France* (revised edn. John Murray, 1981)

Two valuable collections of essays:

L. Brockliss (ed.), *Richelieu and his Age* (Oxford, 1992): see, for example, the essay by D. Parrott, on *'Les Grands* and the Army' and H. Weber on Richelieu's foreign policy.

P.J. Coveney (ed.), *France in Crisis* (Macmillan, 1975): introduces to the student, among other contributions, the work of Mousnier.

Biographies – a selection:

J. Bergin, *Cardinal Richelieu, Power and the Pursuit of Wealth* (Yale, 1985)

R. Kleinman, *Anne of Austria, Queen of France* (Ohio, 1985)

R. J. Knecht, *Richelieu* (Longman, 1991)

Lloyd Moote, *Louis XIII – the Just* (California, 1989)

Geoffrey Treasure, *Mazarin* (Routledge, 1995)

For more ambitious study – a few of the books that have transformed our understanding of the period:

William Beik, *Absolutism and Society in Seventeenth Century France* (Cambridge, 1985)

Y.M. Bercé, *History of Peasant Revolts* (trans. Cornell, 1990)

Richard Bonney, *Political Change in France under Richelieu and Mazarin* (Oxford, 1978)

Julian Dent, *Crisis in Finance: Crown, Financiers and Society in Seventeenth Century France* (David and Charles, 1973)

Sharon Kettering, *Patrons, Brokers and Clients in Seventeenth Century France* (Oxford, 1986)

Lloyd Moote, *The Revolt of the Judges: the Parlement of Paris and the Fronde, 1647–52* (Princeton, 1972)

David Parker, *The Making of French Absolutism* (Arnold, 1983)

Orest Ranum, *Richelieu and the Councillors of Louis XIII* (Oxford, 1963)